Questions and Answers about

Suicide

David Lester

THE CHARLES PRESS, PUBLISHERS
Philadelphia

The Charles Press, Publishers
Post Office Box 15715
Philadelphia, Pennsylvania 19103

Library of Congress Catalog Card Number: 89-060683

ISBN 0-914783-31-9

for Simon

Managing Editor: Sanford Robinson
Editorial Assistant: Sean H. McGlinchey
Compositor: Cage Graphic Arts, Inc.
Designed by Sanford Robinson
Printed in The United States of America

5 4 3 2 1

Contents

Preface

As a professor of psychology whose particular interest (and research) is in suicidal behavior, and as a frequent speaker on the subject throughout the world, I've noticed that many of the questions asked of me by students, the general public, and crisis workers alike, are not topics usually discussed in standard texts on suicide (or, for that matter, in my lectures). Because those questions probably reflect what people actually want to know about suicide, it seemed to me that a collection of questions and answers might serve a very useful purpose, both as a self-sufficient, easy-to-read book, especially for the general reader, and as an adjunct to more formal, scholarly works.

But this is just one reason for using a question-and-answer format. This format has enabled me to present a broad and varied selection of topics without strict adherence to a cental theme. Consequently I have been able to include many subjects that would have been excluded in a more traditional book on suicide. The questions range all the way from the influence of astrology and biorhythms on suicide to fundamental epidemiological and psychiatric issues. Also included are practical questions on how to help a suicidal person and the function and operation of suicide prevention centers.

The answers to the questions have been obtained from the literature, flavored occasionally by my own impressions. I have cited one or more references with each answer so that the reader who desires more information can readily find the key articles or books on the subject. Readers will undoubtedly note that many of the references pertain to research I, myself, have conducted. This is not a form of self-flattery; it simply indicates the product of a lifetime's work in this field.

I sincerely hope this book proves to be of value to all those who want to know more about suicide, especially general readers who have long been influenced by myths and misimpressions about self-destruction. If there are other questions of interest to you about suicide that I have failed to include in this book, please feel free to write to me:

David Lester, Ph.D.
Psychology Program
Richard Stockton State College
Pomona, New Jersey 08240

*Questions and Answers
about Suicide*

Q: Is jumping off buildings a common method for suicide?

A: If we relied on newspaper accounts, movies, and television, it would seem that jumping from buildings is a very common method for suicide, but this is not the case. The media tend to report suicides that are public spectacles, while ignoring less dramatic events. Jumping from a tall structure commands far more attention than, say, committing suicide with sleeping pills. In addition, there are many myths about jumping that are retold so often that they appear as accepted facts. For instance, it is commonly believed that many people jumped from windows to their death after the great stock market crash of 1929. In fact, suicide rates were actually lower in the month following the crash in New York City and in the rest of the country as compared to the previous and following years (Galbraith, 1954). Remarkably, it appears that only one person jumped to his death on Wall Street after the 1929 crash.

This is not to say that jumping to death is truly rare. In cities with a large number of tall buildings, such as Hong Kong, many people do commit suicide by jumping to their death. Recently, Lester and Jason (1989) noted that three of the seven suicides that have taken place at the casinos in Atlantic City were by jumping.

Overall, in the United State in 1985, 721 people (out of a total of 29,453 suicides) jumped to their death. Of these suicides, 293 people jumped from residential premises, 316 from other man-made structures, and 26 from natural sites (86 were unspecified).

References

Galbraith, J. K. *The Great Crash 1929.* Boston: Houghton-Mifflin, 1954.
Lester D., and Jason, D. Suicides at the casinos. *Psychological Reports,* 1989, 64:337-338.

Q: Do you have to be mentally ill to commit suicide or can suicide be a rational act?

A: This is one of the most common questions asked about suicide, and one of the most difficult to answer.

First, very few suicides have received a psychiatric evaluation prior to their deaths. Thus, the exact mental status of those who commit suicide at the time of the event is seldom known.

Psychiatrists have tried retrospectively to assess and diagnose the suicide's psychiatric state prior to the suicide by interviewing family, friends, and co-workers. This method is highly unreliable since the information is second hand and wholly subjective. Nevertheless, it has provided estimates of the percentage of suicides who are psychiatrically disturbed, ranging from five to 94 percent (Temoche, et al., 1964). At least one psychiatrist, Robins (1981) concluded, often looking back at their lives, that most suicides are psychiatrically disturbed. Psychiatrists cannot "forget" that the person they are trying to diagnose died of suicide. Because they rarely try to diagnose non-suicidal people after their death for comparison purposes, the conclusions may be erroneous. (Perhaps many normal people would be judged disturbed by this retrospective method of diagnosis.)

Second, a psychiatric episode may occur acutely. Thus, a suicidal person may not be psychiatrically disturbed a week or even a day prior to his suicide, but we do not know whether his psychiatric state changed just a few hours prior to death.

Another way to answer the question is to prospectively follow a group of patients being tested for specific psychiatric disorders and determine their subsequent suicide rate. Studies that have done this have found psychiatric patients to have higher rates of suicide than non-patients (Sletten, et al., 1972). In Sletten's study the rate of suicide within a year of release from the hospital was highest for those with neurotic depression (830 per 100,000 per year) and psychotic depression (190), and lowest for those with organic brain syndromes (40) and mental retardation (20).

There has also been considerable discussion of whether suicide can be a rational act (for example, Pretzel, 1968). This is a difficult question to answer. We can ask ourselves whether the suicidal person's premises seemed rational and if the conclusion to commit suicide logically followed this premise. However, this begs the real question since suicide is based on personal evaluations of life and death, and what may be irrational to one person may be rational to another.

When we try to answer this question, we too become subjective. If we think that suicide might be a reasonable choice for ourselves under certain conditions, we tend to believe that suicide can be rational. If we would never consider suicide under any conditions, we tend to label suicide as an irrational behavior.

Similarly, the events and precipitants which would drive us to suicide are seen as rational reasons. For example, a person might conceive of himself committing suicide if he had terminal cancer and was in real pain. Therefore, he would judge suicides performed under similar circumstances as rational. However, he probably would not set fire to himself in public to bring about social change (as some people did to protest the Vietnam War in the 1970s). Thus, he would probably view these suicides as irrational.

Each of us, therefore, must make his own decision on this issue.

References

Pretzel, P. W. Philosophical and ethical considertions of suicide prevention. *Bulletin of Suicidology,* 1968, July: 30-38.

Robins, E. *The final months.* New York: Oxford University Press, 1981.

Sletten, I., Brown, M., Evenson, R., and Altman, H. Suicide in mental hospital patients. *Diseases of the Nervous System,* 1972, 33:328-334.

Temoche, A., Pugh, T. F., and MacMahon, B. Suicide rates among current and former mental institution patients. *Journal of Nervous and Mental Disease,* 1964, 138:124-130.

3

Q: *Do teenagers today have a high suicide rate?*
Is it getting higher?

A: The problem of teenage suicide has received increasing attention. It is important to note that this concern does indeed reflect a definite upward trend in teenage suicide rates. Maris (1985) has documented the rise since 1960 for those aged 15 to 24 in the United States (per 100,00 per year) as follows:

	White males	White females	Black males	Black females
1960	8.6	2.3	4.1	1.3
1970	13.9	4.2	10.5	3.8
1980	21.4	4.6	12.3	2.3

It is evident that the suicide rate of each race-by-sex group has increased during the past two decades. Suicide is now the second leading cause of death, after accidents, among the young.

Lester (1988) has recently examined changes in the suicide rates of young people around the world and found that not all nations have experienced this rise. From 1970 to 1980, some countries (like Australia and Greece) experienced a rise only in the male youth suicide rate, some (like Chile and Portugal) only in the female youth suicide rate, while others (like Sweden and Venezuela) experienced a *decrease* in the youth suicide rates of both males and females.

In seeking to explain these changes in the youth suicide rate, Maris noted that adolescence is a life crisis that is difficult for today's youth. Modern society has prolonged the stage of adolescence because there is so much to teach the young before they are prepared for adulthood. As a result, the period of marginality, confusion, and ambiguity has been drawn out. Accordingly, teenagers have high rates of unemployment, illegitimate births, drug use, and delinquency.

Teenage suicides are similar to adult suicides in their association with high levels of depression and hopelessness, their social isolation, and increasing use of firearms. Teenagers differ in being more likely to see suicide as a solution for interpersonal problems and to be more impulsive in their suicidal ehavior.

Jacobs (1971) noted that suicidal teenagers typically come from very disorganized homes. They experience not only broken homes, but a long-standing history of problems of which the broken home is but one. Their parents tend to have many divorces, and the relationships between the parents and the suicidal teenagers is considerably worse than that between parents and nonsuicidal teenagers. The suicidal teenagers also showed more behavioral problems, especially involving withdrawal (such as running away). Their relationship with their parents was characterized by much friction, and they felt more alienated from them. Many suicidal teenagers are of course psychiatrically disturbed as well.

Today, research is beginning to focus on child abuse and how this may increase the likelihood of subsequent suicide. For example, Nilson (1981) found that runaway children were more likely to have experienced abuse and neglect and more likely to have attempted suicide than children referred by county agencies for other types of problems.

References

Jacobs, J. *Adolescent suicide.* New York: Wiley, 1971.
Lester, D. Youth suicide: a cross-cultural perspective, *Adolescence,* 1988, 23:955-958.
Maris, R. The adolescent suicide problem. *Suicide and Life-Threatening Behavior,* 1985, 15:91-108.
Nilson, P. Psychological profiles of runaway children and adolescents. In C. F. Wells & J. R. Stuart (Eds.) *Self-destructive behavior in children and adolescents.* New York: Van Nostrand Reinhold, 1981, 2-43.

Q: *What are the main motives for suicide?*

A: When the question is asked why people commit suicide, it usually refers to the events that may have precipitated the act, rather than the real motivation for taking one's life. There are many critical situations in life that may precipitate suicide, but these are not *underlying causes*. For example, a person may commit suicide soon after the death of a spouse, after the loss of a job, after finding out he has cancer, after being jilted by a lover, after being arrested for a crime, or various other events.

What is interesting about such precipitants is that they provide very unsatisfactory answers to the question of why people kill themselves. For example, divorce is very common in America: typically, one partner walks out on the other. If all deserted spouses killed themselves, there would be a dramatic decline in the population. The vast majority of deserted spouses do not commit suicide but live on.

The situation is similar with terminal illnesses. Although finding out that one has a terminal illness may occasionally precipitate suicide in individuals, almost all such terminal patients die from their illness. Relatively few terminally ill people commit suicide.

In all, researchers have shown little interest in the precipitants for suicide, with one exception: the observation that suicidal behavior in teenagers and young adults is more likely to be precipitated by interpersonal events, whereas in older people the precipitants are more likely to be personal (such as physical pain or severe depression).

Instead, research has focused on the major themes in suicidal behavior. Menninger (1938) described three main motives for suicide: to die, to kill, and to be killed.

To Die: People who want to die usually suffer from unbearable physical or psychological pain and want to escape from it. Others may desire death so that they can be reunited with a loved one already deceased.

To Kill: Some people are extremely angry, usually with loved ones, and express this anger in their suicide attempt. They may focus on the shame that will be attached to their relatives after the suicide. Or they may hope to make the survivors suffer with guilt and remorse. This is illustrated by those who shoot themselves (especially in the head) in front of loved ones and by those who kill themselves in such a way that loved ones will discover their mutilated bodies.

To Be Killed: People who commit suicide are usually depressed. In extreme depression (especially if it is of psychotic proportions) the suicidal person may feel worthless, wicked, evil, and sinful (even though an objective observer may judge the person to be reasonably normal). These people often view suicide as an act of atonement, as a way of making up for all the trouble they believe they have caused others.

Menninger noted that these motives are usually not found independently, but rather in combination.

Reference

Menninger, K. *Man against himself.* New York: Harcourt, Brace and World, 1938.

Q: Why do some people repeatedly attempt suicide?

A: There is a group of suicide attempters who make multiple attempts at suicide. Among the celebrities who have killed themselves, Judy Garland and Marilyn Monroe both made repeated attempts at suicide before finally dying from drug overdoses.

However, those who attempt suicide but do not complete it seem to be in a separate category. In Britain, investigators no longer refer to attempted suicides as such. They use the terms *parasuicides* and, more recently, *self-injurers* or *self-poisoners* in order to indicate that suicidal motivation is often lacking in attempted suicides, particularly in those who repeat the attempt. It has been shown, for instance, that some individuals take only half of what they know is a lethal dose of medication and do so on many separate occasions.

It has been noted that those who make repeated attempts at suicide are more socially deviant in general than other suicidal persons. They are more likely to be alcohol and drug abusers, more likely to have been arrested, more likely to receive a psychiatric diagnosis of psychopathy or other personality disorder, and more likely to come from a socially disorganized part of town.

It is, however, far from clear at present why these people have chosen repeated attempts at suicide, rather than some other behavior, as a means of manipulating their environment or changing their psychological state. A study of self-mutilation in disturbed children many years ago showed that self-mutilation was more common when verbal skills were absent. The children who could talk were able to ventilate their feelings by speech and writing, rather than through self-destructive behavior. By analogy, perhaps those who attempt suicide repeatedly do not have the skills to identify and execute non-destructive tactics.

Reference

Lester, D. *Suicide as a learned behavior.* Springfield: Thomas, 1987.

Q: *Do many suicides leave notes?*

A: The suicide note is a very important piece of information for students of suicide because completed suicides leave very little information behind to explain their motives. Few have been hospitalized or examined by a psychiatrist, and those that have been examined have been given a variety of psychological assessment tests. The recollections of friends and relatives are often distorted by the knowledge that the person has killed himself. Therefore, the suicide note offers an important lead in understanding suicide.

Estimates of the proportion of completed suicides who leave notes varies from 10 to 25 percent in different studies. However, in a thorough study of Los Angeles County in 1957, Shneidman and Farberow (1961) found that 35 percent of men and 39 percent of women who killed themselves left notes. For those attempting suicide, only two percent of men and one percent of women left notes. (These percentages for attempted suicides are undoubtedly underestimates since presumably most notes left by attempters are destroyed before they are discovered by the authorities.)

Do note writers and those who do not write notes differ? At least with regard to simple social characteristics, the answer is no. For example, Tuckman, et al. (1960) found no differences in age, race, sex, employment status, marital status, physical condition, psychiatric condition, or a history of prior suicidal behavior between the two groups.

What about those who write multiple notes? Tuckman and Ziegler (1968) found that writers of more than one note were more likely to be divorced or separated, referred to others more in their notes, and communicated more negative and more ambivalent emotions.

References

Shneidman, E. S., and Farberow, N. L. Statistical comparisons between committed and attempted suicide. In N. L. Farberow and E. S. Shneidman (Eds.) *The cry for help.* New York: McGraw-Hill, 1961, 19-47.

Tuckman, J., Kleiner, R. J., and Lavell, H. Credibility of suicide notes. *American Journal of Psychiatry,* 1960, 116:1104-1106.

Tuckman, J., and Ziegler, R. A comparison of single and multiple note writers. *Journal of Clinical Psychology,* 1968, 24:179-180.

Q: What do suicide notes tell us about the mind of the suicide?

A: The most common type of suicide note tries to reconcile the individual's image of himself as a trustworthy and rational person with the fact that he is about to kill himself, which looks like the irrational act of an untrustworthy person (Jacobs, 1967).

Suicide notes commonly communicate that the writer is faced with extremely distressing problems that have gone on for a long time and which permit no solution other than death. The writer often indicates that he feels (and perhaps actually is) socially isolated, so that his distress and anguish cannot be shared. Finally, the writer often makes provisions for his protection after death by asking his survivors to forgive him and pray for him and by acknowledging that he knows that his readers will not understand or agree with his choice, although he hopes that God will understand. If the writer has a terminal illness, he may not request forgiveness.

Less common, but still of importance, are notes expressing anger. These notes tend to be brief, to blame others for the individual's misfortune, and to omit a request for forgiveness. Finally, some notes simply consist of instructions about belongings or are last wills and testaments. Such notes are usually quite impersonal.

Notes by older people usually express fewer interpersonal reasons (such as rejection by others) for the suicide, and stress instead the desire to escape pain and loneliness (Darbonne, 1969). Their notes contain more instructions, more justification for the suicide, and less emotion. Married writers express more positive emotions in the notes toward others, while divorced and separated note writers express more hostile emotions. Virtually no differences have been identified between the suicide notes of men and women.

There are also suggestions from research that suicide

notes often avoid mentioning the word suicide and are generally not very explicit about the writer's impending death (Spiegel and Neuringer, 1969). In general, the notes also tend to be quite disorganized.

References

Darbonne, A. R. Suicide and age. *Journal of Consulting and Clinical Psychology,* 1969, 33:46-50

Jacobs, J. A phenomenological study of suicide notes. *Social Problems,* 1967, 15:60-72.

Spiegel, D., and Neuringer, C. Role of dread in suicidal behavior. *Journal of Abnormal and Social Psychology,* 1963, 66:507-511.

Q: *What is a suicidal crisis?*

A: Experience has shown that people rarely remain seriously suicidal for long periods of time. Generally, what seems to happen is that the level of stress, regardless of its origin or nature, increases to a point where the resulting distress is so severe that suicide can become an option. However, such high levels of mental distress cannot be endured for more than a few days; eventually the mind becomes numb to the psychological pain or else the crisis passes. Almost all of the suicide prevention centers and crisis counseling services in the United States base their treatment plan on this premise (Tabachnik, 1970).

A person who survives a suicidal crisis may eventually experience another crisis. However, between crises, the person may be able to function well. When trying to help suicidal people, it is accordingly usually wise to view the suicidal state as a temporary one. Most prevention centers contend that if a severely distressed person can be supported and helped through his present crisis, in a few hours or days, he may become much less distressed and therefore much less of a suicidal risk.

During this period of reduced stress, it is often useful to encourage and help the person obtain professional help so that he can deal with the underlying problems.

Unfortunately, this model does not apply to everyone; there is a small group of suicidal people who appear to be chronically suicidal. For example, some alcoholics are chronically depressed and may actually threaten suicide every day. On any one day, the risk that they will kill themselves in quite low, but compounded day after day, the risk becomes much higher. As Wold and Litman (1973) have pointed out, this type of person is often the most difficult to help. Agencies frequently do not have the resources to deal with them, and friends and relatives often tire of them and develop feelings of hostility.

References

Tabachnick, N. The crisis treatment of suicide. *California Medicine,* 1970, 112(June):1-8.

Wold, C., and Litman, R. E. Suicide after contact with a suicide prevention center. *Archives of General Psychiatry,* 1973, 28:735-739.

Q: *What should you do if a friend threatens to commit suicide?*

A: It is only natural to feel acute anxiety when faced with the possibility that a friend is seriously suicidal. What could be more frightening than feeling that you alone may be the barrier between the life and death of a person? What if your fear, distress, or inexperience causes you to say the wrong thing and your friend actually kills himself?

Knowing how to deal with a situation as delicate as a person threatening suicide is crucial, since the correct method of intervention could possibly save a life. First, however, it is essential to realize that anyone has the right to kill himself, and despite your most persuasive attempt to help the person, he can always walk away from you and carry out the suicide elsewhere. In other words, there is often nothing you can do to help, and suicide could occur regardless of your efforts.

This does not mean that you should not try to help; remember, there is always the chance that you *could* save a person's life, especially if you know just a little about how to do it.

The first step is to be receptive to the person. This means listening thoughtfully and allowing the person to ventilate his thoughts and feelings. Second, it is essential to know how great the risk of suicide really is; you must find out as much as possible about the extent of the suicidal thoughts. How long has the person been suicidal? Does he have a "plan" for suicide, and, if so, has he already obtained the necessary means for carrying out this plan?

Once you have some idea of how strong the suicidal intent is, you can turn to the critical issue: what has happened to make the person feel this way? Why is he depressed or anxious? What stressful events have happened recently? It is important to listen carefully since this may be the one best way to help.

Listening is not a simple task, mainly because we do not always hear what is really being said. A good way to orient yourself toward listening is to question whether or not you really comprehend what your friend is telling you. Do you understand what he is actually trying to convey? Try to confirm your impressions: "Let me make sure I am understanding you. What you are telling me is that this happened and as a result you feel like this? Is this right?" Let the person correct you and encourge him to elaborate and amplify his feelings. Ask if anything else is troubling him. Let him tell you what is going on in his mind while you listen carefully.

Remember, the imminence of a suicidal act is only part of the overall problem; to concentrate on this alone will only make you anxious. It is therefore important to look to the events that precipitated the suicidal feelings. The underlying problem may be illness, alcoholism, loneliness, or the death of a loved one. These are the issues that need to be ventilated and your goal is to urge the person to discuss these problems, to calm him down, and, ultimately, to get him through the crisis.

Once a person gets past the immediate crisis and the desire to kill himself, it is wise to suggest seeking professional help for long-term counseling. Perhaps the person could benefit from psychotherapy. Although it is easy enough to advise someone to call a psychiatrist or psychologist and to make an appointment, it is, unfortunately, very hard to get the person to follow through. Even for professionals, this can often be the most difficult part of helping others.

Q: *Are those who threaten suicide or make suicide gestures really suicidal?*

A: It is commonly believed that those who threaten suicide or who make mild attempts or gestures at suicide are not really suicidal, and perhaps we should not be too concerned about them. Indeed, we often feel quite angry and hostile toward them for trying to manipulate us and for wasting our time.

This is one of the most common myths about suicide. The fact is that those who exhibit suicidal behaviors, even in mild ways, are serious suicidal risks. If a person is contemplating suicide now or has attempted suicide in the past, his potential for killing himself is substantially increased.

Let us look at some figures to substantiate this conclusion. About one percent of all deaths in the United States are from suicide. For those who have made a suicide attempt, 15 percent will eventually die from suicide. Thus, the likelihood of a death from suicide is 15 times higher for suicide attempters. Remember, the death may not occur within a week, a month, or even a year. But, eventually, suicidal deaths will occur in a significant number of suicide attempters. On the other hand, we could look at this figure and conclude that the majority of suicide attempters (85%) will die from causes other than suicide. This thinking obscures the scope of the problem.

The best way to view potential suicide is similar to the way we view a serious medical illness such as cancer. For cancer, we undergo a series of tests to see whether we have the disease or are at high risk to develop it. These diagnostic studies are meant to be overcautious, slanted in favor of identifying even false positives. It is better if the test identifies more people as having cancer than really do, rather than failing to identify people who in fact have cancer (false negatives).

The situation is similar with suicide. It is better to over-estimate the risk of suicide in a friend, relative, or client or to judge the potential to be there when it is not, and to respond accordingly (even if this means being "taken for a ride" or being manipulated on occasion) rather than ignore the risk of suicide in someone who later does commit suicide.

Reference

Dorpat, T. L. and Ripley, H. S. The relationship between attempted suicide and completed suicide. *Comprehensive Psychiatry* 1967, 8:74-89.

Q: *Where can you get help immediately for a suicidal person?*

A: The quickest and usually most dependable way to obtain help for a suicidal person is to call the nearest suicide prevention center or crisis counseling service. These facilities are available in most cities or regional areas and are listed in the telephone directory, usually in the white pages under "Suicide Prevention Centers." In some cities, suicide centers are listed under "Crisis Intervention Networks." (Unfortunately, crisis intervention is a generic term and may mean a crisis counseling center for suicidal persons, or a crisis service to handle disasters such as floods, fires, and similar catastrophes.) Suicide prevention centers are often identified conspicuously on the inner front cover of the telephone directory, along with the emergency numbers for the police and fire departments. The yellow pages seldom list suicide prevention centers.

Suicidal persons who are not in a crisis state are often referred by the suicide prevention center to other facilities for counseling or psychotherapy. The selection of a counselor or therapist is influenced by the resources available within the community and by the person's financial status. Finding the best counselor or therapist for a particular individual can be challenging because there is considerable variation among professionals in orientation and therapeutic approaches.

Q: *What do suicide prevention centers do and are they successful?*

A: Suicide prevention centers were rare in the 1960s, but today most communities have a suicide prevention center or crisis counseling center. There is no uniformity among the centers. Some are sponsored by mental health agencies, some by churches and others by community groups.

Most centers are oriented around a telephone counseling service which is open 24 hours a day, 7 days a week. A depressed or suicidal person can call the center and talk to a counselor who is typically a paraprofessional—someone who is not a qualified psychologist, psychiatrist or social worker, but rather a volunteer from the community who has received twenty to thirty hours of training in crisis counseling.

Counselors usually explore a caller's psychological state and assist in devising a plan of action, although some centers do not permit their counselors to offer advice, allowing them only to listen actively to clients.

A few centers have developed more active services that will dispatch qualified mental health workers to visit clients in the community. Some centers contact people at high risk for suicide (such as those who have attempted suicide and survivors of suicide) and offer counseling. Other centers maintain walk-in clinics for clients and run support groups for those who have had a loved one commit suicide. These self-help groups are becoming common throughout the country.

Current research has failed to document that suicide prevention centers have significant impact on the suicide rates of the communities they serve (Lester, 1988). This is not surprising since suicide is so rare. On the other hand, it is generally agreed that the centers do an excellent job of crisis intervention. In addition most centers are well acquainted with the resources in their communities and can assist clients in obtaining help from appropriate community agencies.

The American Association of Suicidology (2459 South Ash, Denver, CO 80222) has set up standards for suicide prevention centers and inspects and certifies centers. A list of certified centers can be obtained from the association.

Reference

Lester, D. *Can we prevent suicide?* New York: AMS, 1989.

Q: What kind of training do suicide prevention counselors receive?

A: Suicide prevention centers vary widely in the personnel they use to provide crisis counseling. Some centers are located in mental health agencies and utilize psychiatrists, psychologists, social workers, and psychiatric nurses who are well trained in general counseling techniques and who have received additional training in crisis counseling, but suicide prevention centers of this type are rare.

The majority of centers in the United States use *paraprofessionals* as counselors. These individuals are recruited from the community, usually volunteers who are interviewed and screened. They receive about 25 to 30 hours of training in active listening (or, in technical terms, client-centered therapy), dealing with crises, along with some basic information about suicide and the social resources available in the community. These crisis counselors are usually helpful only for the crisis itself. It is unlikely that crisis counselors can achieve substantial changes in a client's life that will prevent suicidal crises from recurring. On the other hand, the service provided by paraprofessional counselors can be invaluable at the time of the crisis.

After a crisis has been resolved, crisis counselors face the task of attempting to motivate clients to enter long-term psychotherapy in order to prevent recurrent episodes. In many ways this role is as important as managing the crisis.

Reference

Lester, D., and Brockopp, G. W. *Crisis intervention and counseling by telephone.* Springfield: Thomas, 1973.

Q: *Once a suicidal person visits a psychotherapist, what can the therapist do?*

A: The first thing a psychotherapist does is assess the self-destructiveness of the client. Does he need immediate hospitalization? Does he need some other form of treatment, such as antidepressant drugs? How urgent is the situation?

What is the best psychotherapeutic approach to a suicidal client? The answer has varied greatly over the years. There are schools and trends in psychotherapy, and some psychotherapies are better suited to certain clients than others. Today, the most popular psychotherapies are the cognitive therapies, such as Albert Ellis' rational-emotive therapy, Aaron Beck's cognitive therapy, and William Glasser's reality therapy, all of which focus on changing the client's irrational ways of thinking and viewing the world. These therapies help clients resolve their depression and anxiety and plan strategies and tactics for achieving what they want.

Cognitive psychotherapies are also excellent for those who are not comfortable with psychiatry and might be suspicious of going to see a therapist. Cognitive therapists tend to avoid medication, psychoanalysis, and the expressive approaches of the 1960s (such as gestalt therapy), which sometimes alienate those not familiar with modern psychotherapeutic techniques. Cognitive therapies are well-suited for a high percentage of suicidal individuals and are probably the most widely used techniques at present.

Q: *Why is suicide more common after a psychiatric patient is released from the hospital?*

A: There are many factors which change for the worse after a psychiatric patient is released from the hospital, despite the fact that in order to be released the patient's ability to function must have improved.

In some ways, life is simple in the psychiatric hospital. The patient no longer has to deal with family members, difficult social relationships, or the stresses of work. In effect, psychiatric hospitals provide relief from the stresses of daily life. After release, the ex-patient has to face all of the stresses which probably played a part in the original psychiatric breakdown.

While in the hospital, the staff make sure that patients take their medication and, if there is a risk of suicide, carefully monitor them to ensure that they do not kill themselves. After release from the hospital, patients are often reluctant to take their medication (which often has unpleasant side effects). And there are many more opportunities for them to kill themselves in a non-protected environment.

Suicide is most likely in those who have affective disorders, especially those who are severely depressed. It may well be that people do not have enough energy to plan and execute their own suicide when deeply depressed. However, as they come out of the depression, they may feel sufficiently energized to kill themselves. This increase in energy level is often interpreted as a sign of improvement. Therefore, patients may be released once their depression lifts, but before they have returned to a normal life-supporting frame of mind. This fact, combined with having to confront the stresses of life once more and without the careful monitoring of their behavior by others, can make the period after hospital release the most dangerous for suicide.

Reference

Sletten, I., Brown, M., Evenson, R., and Altman, H. Suicide in mental hospital patients. *Diseases of the Nervous System,* 1972, 33:328-334.

Q: *Can we predict who will commit suicide?*

A: The Los Angeles Suicide Prevention Center devised a simple questionnaire in the 1960s for telephone crisis counselors to use to predict the relative suicidal risk clients posed. The questions assess five characteristics, each of which is scored from one to nine; these are averaged to provide an overall suicide potential rating. A simplified version of the questionnaire has been presented by Lester (1986). The five key characteristics and their scoring are as follows:

Characteristic one assesses age and sex. The highest score (7-9) is given to men 50 years and older, and the lowest score (1-3) to women of any age. The reason for this is that elderly white males have the highest suicide rate of all demographic groups.

Characteristic two assesses psychiatric symptoms. People with severe depression receive the highest score (7-9), closely followed by those showing symptoms of schizophrenia, such as disorganization, confusion, chaos, delusions, hallucinations, loss of contact, and disorientation (5-8). At the other end of the scale, those with psychosomatic illnesses, such as asthma and ulcers, are given low scores (1-4). Depression is undoubtedly the most common warning sign for suicide.

Characteristic three assesses recent stress. The more stress a person has experienced in recent months, the higher the potential for suicide.

Characteristic four assesses prior and current suicidal thoughts. People inexperienced in dealing with suicidal individuals are often afraid to ask about suicidal intentions, fearing that the questions themselves may precipitate extreme suicidal behavior. Clinical experience has shown that this does not happen, and that bringing up the question is both safe and sensible. In fact, accurate assessment of a person's suicide potential is impossible without this information.

The person's potential for suicide is higher if he has

attempted suicide in the past; if he is currently considering suicide as an option; if he has a specific plan for suicide and the means are readily available; and if a truly lethal method is contemplated (for example, a gun rather than an overdose of barbiturates).

Characteristic five assesses the personal resources that the person has available and the reactions of his friends and relatives to his condition. An isolated person is at greater risk for suicide, as is someone whose friends and relatives are openly rejecting and hostile.

Interestingly, the use of formal psychological and psychiatric tests does not help us predict the risk that someone will kill himself any better than this simple questionnaire.

Reference

Lester, D. The suicidal person: recognition and helping. *Police Journal,* 1986, 59:216-221.

Q: What is the profile of the high-risk candidate for suicide?

A: Suicide prevention centers commonly give their counselors-in-training a simple scale which identifies those callers with the highest risk of suicide. Although these scales vary with the type of clinic or the population served by the agency, a widely used scale, devised by the Los Angeles Suicide Prevention Center, identifies the following factors for the highest risks:

- elderly white males
- depression (symptoms or the psychiatric diagnosis)
- has made a prior, lethal suicide attempt and has a plan and available method for suicide at present
- recent experience of acute stressful life events
- has few available resources or has friends/relatives who are hostile and rejecting toward the caller.

When estimating relative risk, an experienced counselor does not simply ask only those questions that will enable him or her to fill out the scale and obtain a risk rating. Rather, the necessary information is acquired as the client and counselor talk and as the counselor explores what is going on in the client's world. Sometimes, especially with regard to a history of prior suicidal behavior and current suicidal thoughts, the counselor may inquire directly about these issues if they have not come up naturally in the course of the conversation.

However, it is easy to misuse any scale of suicidal risk by placing too much emphasis on single factors. For example, a counselor does not minimize the suicidal intent or risk of a black, teenage female merely because she is not in the top risk category (elderly, white male). It is important to assess all factors and to weight them according to clinical insight and judgment (which, at its best, is a product of experience with hundreds of clients in crisis).

A word of caution: For those counselors with limited experience, it is always best to anticipate that a caller may commit suicide—even if it seems unlikely—rather than to dismiss the possibility in someone who later does commit suicide.

Reference

Lester, D. The suicidal person: recognition and helping. *Police Journal,* 1986, 59:216-221.

Q: *Does suicide run in families?*

A: The simple answer to this question is, yes, occasionally suicide does appear to run in families. The difficulty comes in interpreting the implications of this fact.

Let us look at an example of a suicidal family (Lester, 1987). Ernest Hall was dying and suffering extreme pain in 1905 after a life in business. He tried to shoot himself, but his son-in-law had taken the bullets out of his gun. The son-in-law, Ed Hemingway, was a doctor, and in 1928 he found out that he himself had severe diabetes. He was depressed and had suffered financial losses. He killed himself one day with a handgun while home for lunch.

Ed had six children, one of whom was Ernest Hemingway, later the Nobel prize-winning writer, who at age 62 also shot himself to death. He too was suffering from a variety of physical illnesses and, in addition, had become psychotic. His youngest brother, Leicester Hemingway, the first person to find his father dead in 1928, had idolized his brother Ernest, who killed himself in 1961. Leicester developed diabetes and underwent five operations, all of which failed to prevent the amputation of his limbs. In 1982, he shot himself with a handgun. One of the four Hemingway sisters, Ursula, killed herself in 1962 with an overdose of drugs while depressed after surviving three cancer operations.

Suicide certainly appears to have run in the Hemingway family, but why? Is it that depression runs in the family? All of the suicides were indeed depressed at the time of their death, although only Ernest appears to have been diagnosed as psychotic.

Is suicide genetic? Perhaps, but there is no real proof of this. Alternatively, could this family reflect the role of learning in suicide behavior? The Hemingways seems to have learned that when you are old, depressed, and suffering from a severe illness, suicide is an acceptable and, perhaps, a preferred solution.

That suicide runs in some families raises the possibility

of a genetic basis for suicidal behavior (or psychiatric illness) and also suggests a learning basis, but there is insufficent evidence to enable us to decide between these two alternatives at the present.

Reference

Lester, D. *Suicide as a learned behavior.* Springfield: Thomas, 1987.

Q: Can suicidal behavior be inherited?

A: One way to study whether a behavior is inherited is to compare identical and non-identical twins. Identical twins have identical genes, whereas non-identical twins share only about 50 percent of their genetic material. Therefore, if identical twins show a greater resemblance in some target behavior than non-identical twins, it suggests that the role of genes may be influential in determining behavior.

On the other hand, identical twins are reared differently from non-identical twins. They are more often dressed alike, confused by relatives, and so on. (Note also that identical twins must be of the same sex, whereas non-identical twins may differ in sex.) Consequently, in studying behavior, investigators try to find identical twins who have been reared separately. Identical twins, however, are rare, and identical twins separated at birth and reared apart are very rare. Identical twins reared apart, one of whom commits suicide, are incredibly rare! Because of this rarity, the results of comparative studies between suicidal identical and non-identical twins may not be reliable.

In a Danish study, however, it was shown that if one identical twin had committed suicide, the probability of the other committing suicide was 21 percent, but for non-identical twins the probability was zero percent (Juel-Nielsen and Videbech, 1970). Thus, according to this single study, identical twins are more likely to resemble each other in suicidal behavior.

However, there is some evidence that psychiatric illness is inherited and that many suicidal people are psychiatrically ill (Lester, 1986). Consequently, determining that genes play a role in suicide may represent a side effect of the heritability of psychiatric ilness, although no study has yet been conducted to test this possibility.

A second sound method for investigating the role of heredity in determining behavior is to study cross-foster offspring, children taken from their natural mothers and raised by foster mothers. Does the child's behavior resemble that of the biological or the adopted mother? For psychiatric illness, there is substantial evidence that a child's psychiatric state resembles that of the biological mother although she has no role in rearing the child or in shaping his social environment. Unfortunately, this type of study has not yet been conducted for suicidal behavior.

Based on the available but limited evidence, it is possible that suicide may be inherited; however, we do not know whether this heritability relates to suicide in particular or to psychiatric illness in general.

References

Juel-Nielsen, N., and Videbech, T. A twin study of suicide. *Acta Geneticae Medicae et Gemellologiae,* 1970, 19:307-310.

Lester, D. Genetics, twin studies, and suicide. *Suicide and Life-Threatening Behavior,* 1986, 16:274-285.

Q: *Is suicide more common in first-borns or last-borns?*

A: Alfred Adler drew the attention of psychologists to the importance of birth order as a source of information about the personalities and life-styles of people. Most parents are well aware of personality differences between their successive children, and several books have appeared detailing the personalities of only children, first-borns, second-born girls, and so on (Forer, 1969).

Researchers into suicide rarely note the birth order of their subjects, but Lester (1987) collected all of the available data from reports that did mention birth order and combined them to provide a sufficient sample. He found that there was an excess of first- and middle-borns in completed suicides and an excess of middle- and last-borns among attempted suicides.

Having identified these trends, it is by no means easy to explain them. The excess of first-borns among completed suicides may be a result of their higher drive to succeed (first-borns appear to be over-represented among high achievers) coupled with subsequent feelings of failure. The excess of last-borns among attempted suicides may be a result of their tendency to develop the habit of manipulating others by means of immature behaviors, tactics learned from being the baby of the family. Such explanations, however, are highly speculative, and no research has yet been conducted on the phenomenon.

References

Forer, L. K. *Birth order and life roles.* Springfield: Thomas, 1969.
Lester, D. Suicide and sibling position. *Individual Psychology,* 1987, 43:390-395.

Q: *Does the risk of suicide increase in children if a parent commits suicide?*

A: Suicide appears to run in some families. This raises the question of whether the loss of a parent by suicide increases the risk of suicide in the children.

The American Association of Suicidology and suicide prevention centers throughout the country are greatly concerned with this possibility. Considerable thought is being given to the organization of services for those who survive a suicide, not just for the children, but for all the relatives. The proceedings of the 20th Annual Meeting of the American Association of Suicidology included 20 papers on this particular topic (Yufit, 1988).

A review of research in the 1970s showed four studies reporting an excess of suicide in the friends and relatives of suicidal people, and four other studies which reported no excess (Lester, 1983). Few studies have focused on suicide just in parents, and the answer, therefore, is uncertain.

The suicide of a parent suggests both the possibility of an inherited predisposition to psychiatric illness in the family or teaching a life style to the next generation that involves self-destructive behavior as a solution for stress. In either case, counseling is critically important for the survivors of a suicide.

References

Lester, D. *Why people kill themselves.* Springfield: Thomas, 1983.
Yufit, R. I. (Ed.) *Proceedings of the 20th Annual Conference of the American Association of Suicidology.* Denver: AAS, 1988.

Q: *Are people more likely to kill themselves on Christmas and other major national holidays?*

A: It is commonly believed that depression is more likely and more intense during Christmas and on other major national holidays, which are seen as times when family and friends get together. Research, however, does not support this belief. For example, Lester (1979) found in the 1970s an average of 61 suicides on the six major national holidays) New Year's Day, Memorial Day, Independence Day, Labor Day, Thanksgiving Day, and Christmas Day) in contrast to 69 suicides the seven days before and after the holidays. In contrast, homicides were more likely on national holidays than at other times (perhaps because these are times when people socialize and consume alcohol).

Thus, the notion that lonely and isolated people are particularly subject to depression on national holidays is not supported by data on suicide rates.

Along these same lines, Lester (1985) found no evidence that people are more likely to kill themselves a few days before or after Christmas, although the number of suicides did show a tendency to increase slightly from December 18 to January 7.

References

Lester, D. Temporal variation in suicide and homicide. *American Journal of Epidemiology,* 1979, 109:517-520.
Lester, D. Suicide at Christmas. *American Journal of Psychiatry,* 1985, 142:782.

Q: *Do suicidal people feel hopeless?*

A: Depression, the usual forerunner of suicide, is a complex state. Psychiatrist Aaron Beck devised one of the most widely used scales to measure the severity of depression; it includes items about moods (such as guilt, sadness, and anger) and behaviors (such as disturbances in appetite, sleep, and general energy) (Beck, et al., 1961).

Beck became convinced that hopelessness, one component of the depressed state, was most critical in suicidal people. To pursue this idea, he devised a questionnaire specifically to measure this feeling (Beck, et al., 1979). In a series of studies, Beck and his colleagues have shown that scores on the hopelessness scale were much more strongly associated with suicidal behavior than were scores on the depression scale.

Several, but not all, independent research teams have replicated this result. Some critics have argued that the items on the hopelessness scale are biased so that respondents might make socially desirable, rather than honest, responses. However, the validity of Beck's conclusion is generally well accepted.

Beck's notion led him to focus on a form of psychotherapy that attempts to change the pattern of thinking in depressed and suicidal people. Their hopelessness is not rational in most cases and results from distorted patterns of thinking. Beck and his associates have devised a system of psychotherapy that attacks the irrational thinking pattern and replaces it with more rational ideas (Burns, 1980).

References

Beck, A. T., Ward, C. H., Mendelson, M., Mock, J., and Erbaugh, J. An inventory for measuring depression. *Archives of General psychiatry,* 1961, 4:55-63.

Beck, A. T. Weissman, A., Lester, D., and Trexler, L. The measurement of pessimism. *Journal of Consulting and Clinical Psychology,* 1974, 42:861-865.

Burns, D. *Feeling good.* New York: Morrow, 1980.

Q: Do stressful life events increase the risk of suicide?

A: Most popular books on stress management contain a "life events" scale, which the reader can use to determine just how stressful his or her life has been during the past year (for example, Girdano and Everly, 1979). The object is to broadly quantify stress. All kinds of traumatic events are listed and each is assigned a weighted number of stress points. On the Holmes and Rahe (1967) scale, the death of a spouse has a weight of 100 points; divorce, 73; and being fired from work, 47. Marriage adds 50 points; obtaining a house mortgage, 31 points; and Christmas excitement, 12 points. A person who accumulates over 300 points during the last 12 months is at risk to experience stress symptoms. Of course, the score is a simplification, but high stress levels may precipitate serious trouble.

Paykel (1979) found that patients (in psychiatric hospitals) who had attempted suicide had experienced more recent stressful life events than patients who were depressed but had not attempted suicide. The attempted suicides had experienced more undesirable life events, but the same number of desirable life events; more major upsets, but the same number of minor upsets; and more events over which they had no control, but the same number of controlled events. Paykel later replicated these findings with a sample of people living in the community.

Pokorny and Kaplan (1976) compared psychiatric patients who committed suicide after release from a psychiatric hospital with patients who did not later kill themselves. The suicides were more likely to have experienced severe depression at the time of admission to the hospital and stressful life events after release.

On this basis, it appears that both attempted and completed suicides commonly experience negative life events prior to their suicidal acts. Suicide after the experience of stressful life events is probably part of a longer life pattern. For example, Maris and Lazerwitz (1973) studied the lives of a group of people who had killed themselves and found a chain of events beginning with multiproblem families and followed by interpersonal failures leading to downward social mobility, feelings of hopelessness, drug abuse, shame, isolation, coming to see death as an escape, attempting suicide, and finally completing suicide.

References

Girdano, D., and Everly, G. *Controlling stress and tension.* Englewood Cliffs: Prentice-Hall, 1979.

Holmes, T. H., and Rahe, R. H. The social readjustment rating scale. *Journal of Psychosomatic Research,* 1967, 11:213-218.

Maris, R., and Lazerwitz, B. Toward a general theory of self-destruction. Unpublished, 1973.

Paykel, E. Life stress. In L. Hankoff and B. Einsidler (Eds.) *Suicide.* Littleton, MA: PSG, 1979, 225-234.

Pokorny, A. D., and Kaplan, H. Suicide following psychiatric hospitalization. *Journal of Nervous and Mental Disease,* 1976, 162:119-125.

Q: *Do AIDS patients have a high suicide rate?*

A: Several features of AIDS (acquired immunodeficiency syndrome) might increase the risk of suicide. First, it is a terminal illness. Many investigators (but not all) report higher rates of suicide in those with terminal illnesses, such as cancer and Huntington's disease, as well as those undergoing organ transplants or hemodialysis.

Second, AIDS affects certain groups in our society far more than others: homosexuals, minority drug addicts, and those receiving blood transfusions. Estimates vary, but Ansberry (1987) estimated that 65 percent of AIDS patients are homosexual or bisexual men while 17 percent are drug abusers.

Surprisingly, there are no good epidemiological studies of the incidence of suicide in homosexuals, although attempted suicide does appear to be quite common among this group (Lester, 1983). On the other hand, drug abusers appear to have higher death rates, mostly from accidental drug overdoses, but perhaps from suicide as well. Again, accurate estimates of the actual suicide rate are not available (Lester, 1983).

Third, as is common with most terminal illnesses, patients dying from AIDS face enormous stress. There is a great social stigma attached to having AIDS, and AIDS patients often face rejection from friends and professionals (and even physical abuse). Furthermore, most AIDS victims ultimately exhaust their funds and face bankruptcy. AIDS is also accompanied by psychiatric disorders, not only from the stresses just mentioned, but from direct central nervous system involvement by the disease itself. Organic mental disorders are present in about 25 percent of all AIDS patients. Perry and Thomas (1984) found major depressive disorders in 17 percent of a sample of AIDS patients, delirium in 29 percent, dementia in 11 percent, and schizophrenia in 2 percent.

For all of these reasons, suicide may be very common

in AIDS patients, but until 1988, only isolated case studies of suicide in AIDS patients had appeared. Recently, Marzuk, et al. (1988) reported that the suicide rate for male AIDS patients was indeed high: 681 per 100,000 per year in New York City, as compared to 19 for men aged 10-59 without AIDS. In addition, some individuals continue to engage in dangerous sexual activity after learning about AIDS, occasionally even consciously trying to commit suicide by getting AIDS (Frances, et al., 1985).

References

Ansberry, C. AIDS, stirring panic and prejudice, tests the nation's character. *The Wall Street Journal,* 1987, CCX(97), 1:6.
Frances, R. J., Wikstrom, T., and Alcena, V. Contracting AIDS as a means of committing suicide. *American Journal of Psychiatry,* 1985, 142:656.
Lester, D. *Why people kill themselves.* Springfield: Thomas, 1983.
Marzuk, P. M., Turney, H., Tardiff, K., Gross, E. M., Morgan, E. B., Hsu, M. A., and Mann, J. Increased risk suicide in persons with AIDS. *Journal of the American Medical Association,* 1988, 259:1333-1337.
Perry, S. W., and Tross, S. Psychiatric problems of AIDS inpatients at the New York Hospital. *Public Health Reports,* 1984, 99:200-205.

Q: *Does the risk of suicide increase in patients with terminal illness?*

A: It is difficult to make predictions about the risk of suicide in those with terminal illnesses. On one hand, we might expect suicide rates to be high, since the illness is a severe stress for the person. In cases of terminal illness, a person might want to kill himself in order to escape the physical pain and psychological suffering associated with the disease. On the other hand, Henry and Short (1954) have argued that when people have an external source of frustration, such as chronic illness, that accounts for their unhappiness, they are less likely to feel suicidal. It is when there are no external sources of blame that suicide becomes more likely.

Although not all studies are in agreement, most research supports the conclusion that the risk of suicide is greater in patients with cancer (for example, Whitlock, 1978). Suicide also appears more likely in patients on hemodialysis (Haenel, et al., 1980), those who have received transplants (Haenel, et al., 1980), and those who have spinal cord injuries (Le and Price, 1982).

Thus, a common sense prediction, rather than the Henry and Short theory, seems correct. Studies on patients with more serious illnesses generally show a high risk of suicide and a higher percentge of deaths from suicide than in the average person.

It should be noted that many patients with serious diseases can hasten their death by abusing (or by not using) critical medication, by neglecting their diet, by refusing treatment, or by continuing life-threatening behaviors (such as drinking alcohol or smoking). These behaviors are not usually listed as suicidal. Thus, self-destructive behavior leading to death in terminal patients may be more common than reported.

References

Haenel, T., Brunner, F., and Battegay, R. Renal dialysis and suicide. *Comprehensive Psychiatry,* 1980, 21:140-145.

Henry, A. F., and Short, J. F. *Suicide and homicide.* New York: Free Press, 1954.

Le, C., and Price, M. Survival from spinal cord injury. *Journal of Chronic Diseases,* 1982, 35:487-492.

Whitlock, F. Suicide, cancer and depression. *British Journal of Psychiatry,* 1978, 132:269-274.

Q: *Do suicide rates increase after famous people kill themselves?*

A: It had long been felt that reports of famous suicides by the media might lead others to kill themselves, but the phenomenon was not documented accurately until the 1970s. Phillips (1974) studied the impact of suicides that made the front pages of major newspapers and found a rise in the number of suicides in the month following such a suicide story. He studied 33 suicide stories and found a rise in the number of suicides after 26 of them and a decrease after seven of them. Overall, the number of suicides in the following month rose by about 3% (58 more suicides among a total of about 1700 in the month).

Phillips and his associates have published a large number of related studies since that first report. All support and significantly add to his earlier conclusion. For example, after a suicide story, single-car crashes increase, although multi-car crashes do not, suggesting that publicity about suicide may also indirectly influence self-destructive behaviors. Publicity of suicide on television (in soap operas, television news broadcasts, and special suicide programs) has also been followed by an increase in the number of suicides in the following weeks.

More recently, Stack (1987) has reported that this increase in the number of suicides following a suicide story occurs only after the suicide of an entertainment personality or an American politician. Suicides by foreigners, villains, and artists do not result in an increase. There has been some evidence that this "suggestion effect" may be stronger in teenagers than in adults.

Lester (1987) has used these findings, along with the results of other research, to suggest that suicide may be in part a learned behavior. In effect, the publicity about suicide teaches people about when to kill themselvs, how to kill themselves, and why to kill themselves (imitation suicides often use the same method and locale for their suicidal actions). For example, the Buddhist monks who set fire to themselves in the 1970s to protest American involvement in the Vietnam War were followed by self-immolations in the United States and Britain, usually for political motives. Similarly, the dramatic rise in suicides using car exhaust in England and Wales during the 1980s can be seen as the result of the "discovery' of this method of suicide when the English heard about suicides using car exhaust from accounts in the media.

References

Lester, D. *Suicide as a learned behavior.* Springfield: Thomas, 1987.
Phillips, D. The influences of suggestion on suicide. *American Sociological Review,* 1974, 39:340-354.
Stack, S. Celebrities and suicide. *American Sociological Review,* 1987, 52:401-412.

Q: *Why do so many women attempt suicide, but rarely die?*

A: One of the most reliable phenomena in the study of suicide is that men are more likely to complete suicide (that is, to die) than women. In contrast, women are much more likely to attempt suicide (and survive) than men. In one of the best community surveys, in Los Angeles County in 1957, Farberow and Shneidman (1957) identified 540 men and 228 women who completed suicide and 828 men and 1824 women who had attempted suicide. The same phenomenon has been found in surveys in Hong Kong and the Netherlands.

Perhaps the most obvious reason for this sex difference is that men and women choose different methods for suicide. Men are more likely to use firearms and hanging, whereas women are more likely to use poisons and medication. Furthermore, when using firearms, men are more likely to shoot themselves in the head, whereas women are more likely to shoot themselves in the body. In all, the methods used by men are more lethal, that is, death is more likely to result from these actions, and there is less opportunity to change one's mind about dying after shooting oneself than there is after, say, taking an overdose of pills.

What accounts for this difference in choice of method (high lethality versus low lethality) for suicide? Perhaps women are less intent on dying, but are using the suicidal act as a way of manipulating others. On the other hand, there is evidence that women are more concerned with their bodily appearance after death, and consequently choose less disfiguring methods for suicide, which incidentally are also less lethal.

But the issue is more complicated than just the lethality of the method selected. Lester (1984) has shown that, within any one method for suicide, men are still more likely to die than women. Therefore, differences in choice of method cannot be the sole explanation for the sex difference in the outcome of suicidal actions.

Other possible explanations for the sex difference have been proposed. It has been suggested that men have higher rates of psychosis than women, and psychotics are more likely to complete suicide than people with other psychiatric diagnoses. Also, suicide attempts in women seem to vary in frequency at different times during the menstrual cycle, suggesting the possibility of hormonal factors in suicidal behavior. Then, too, there is a societal labelling of suicidal actions, in which completed suicide is viewed as "masculine" while attempted suicide is seen as "feminine." This perception may affect the likelihood of men and women choosing between the two behaviors when in distress.

References

Farberow, N. L., and Shneidman, E. S. *The cry for help.* New York: McGraw-Hill, 1961.

Lester, D. Suicide. In C. S. Widom (Ed.) *Sex roles and psychopathology.* New York: Plenum, 1984, 145-156.

Q: *Is suicide more common premenstrually?*

A: It has been noted that suicidal behavior differs in men and women. Men have higher rates of completed suicide, while women have higher rates of attempted suicide.

The question arises whether suicidal behavior in women varies with the phases of the menstrual cycle. Opinions about the premenstrual syndrome itself have changed over the years. Through the 1960s, the prevailing view was that premenstrual changes in mood were psychologically induced. It was thought that women *expected* to be irritable or depressed premenstrually and developed these moods as a result of their expectations. By the late 1980s, opinion had switched: it is now believed that changes in mood over the menstrual cycle are valid and are quite possibly due to physiological, rather than psychological, causes.

Studies of suicidal behavior have shown that attempted suicide is more common in the premenstrual and bleeding phases of the cycle, and perhaps also during ovulation (Tonks, et al., 1968). However, not all research studies confirm this finding. Only one study has appeared on completed suicide, and this reported an increase during ovulation (McKinnon, et al., 1959).

Lester (1988) has speculated on the possible physiological mechanisms by which the sex hormones could affect suicidal behavior, concluding that more studies are required before we can place confidence in the validity of an association between the menstrual cycle and suicidal behavior.

References

Lester, D. *The biochemical basis of suicide.* Springfield: Thomas, 1988.
McKinnon, I. L., McKinnon, P., and Thomson, A. D. Lethal hazards of the luteal phase of the menstrual cycle. *British Medical Journal,* 1959, 1:1015.
Tonks, C. M., Rack, P. H. and Rose, M. J. Attempted suicide and the menstrual cycle. *Journal of Psychosomatic Research,* 1968, 2:319-327.

Q: What is the suicide rate in pregnant women?

A: It has commonly been reported that the suicide rate in pregnant women is quite low. Barno (1967) estimated the suicide rate to be only 0.03 per 100,000 per year (as compared to about 6 or 7 per 100,000 per year in American women generally). Lewis and Fay (1981) examined 2.3 million births and found six ante-partum completed suicides and eleven post-partum.

Attempted suicide is far more common than completed suicide during pregnancy. Whitlock and Edwards (1968) reviewed data on the number of pregnant women among samples of attempted suicides and concluded that the best estimate was six percent. Attempted suicide appears to be less common in the third trimester than in the first two trimesters. In 30 cases of pregnant women who had attempted suicide, the pregnancy was thought to play a role in 13 cases.

More recently, Lester and Beck (1988) found no differences in the level of depression or hopelessness of pregnant and non-pregnant women who had attempted suicide. The pregnancy appeared to play a role in the suicide attempt for 53 percent of the women, and three themes were common among the pregnant women: prior loss of children (by miscarriage, adoption, or death), potential loss of their lover, and the desire for an abortion.

References

Barno, A. Criminal abortion deaths, illegitimate pregnancy deaths and suicides in pregnancy. *American Journal of Obstetrics and Gynecology,* 1967, 98:356-367.
Lester, D., and Beck, A. T. Attempted suicide and pregnancy. *American Journal of Obstetrics and Gynecology,* 1988, 158:1084-1085.
Lewis, G., and Fay, R. Suicide in pregnancy. *British Journal of Clinical Practice,* 1981, 35:51-53.
Whitlock, F., and Edwards, J. Pregnancy and attempted suicide. *Comprehensive Psychiatry,* 1968, 9:1-12.

Q: Do working women have higher rates of suicide?

A: In keeping with the equal opportunity movement in recent years, women have entered the labor force in greater numbers and have had greater access to the professions. Has this change affected their suicide rate?

An increased suicide rate might be due to the fact that working women experience increased role conflict. Not only must they succeed in traditional roles as women, but also they must now succeed in their careers. (For example, although more women have entered professions formerly dominated by men, far fewer men have chosen to modify their life styles by taking over more of the tasks formerly carried out by women homemakers.)

Alternatively, it may be that certain careers lead to an increased risk of suicide because of the particular kinds of stresses they involve. For instance, the stress involved in a career may open a person more to conflict of success versus failure—a stress that appears to be a major factor underlying the motives of suicide in Japan and Sweden. (Note, this viewpoint does not argue that housework is unstressful. Rather, it suggests that the stress experienced by the traditional homemaker does not increase her risk of suicide.)

Recent research does indeed show that suicide rates in women who are physicians, psychologists, nurses, and chemists may be high, perhaps as high as those of men in these professions (Mausner and Steppacher, 1973; Ross, 1973).

However, Cumming, et al. (1975) compared married women in Canada who were employed with those who were not employed and found that the employed women had a *lower* suicide rate. This finding suggests that working in general does not lead to an increased risk of suicide. Instead, it is the pursuit of a professional career that may increase the risk of suicide in women.

References

Cumming, E., Lazer, C., and Chisholm, L. Suicide as an index of role strain among employed and not-employed married women in British Columbia. *Canadian Review of Sociology and Anthropology,* 1975, 12:462-470.

Mausner, J., and Steppacher, R. Suicide in professionals. *American Journal of Epidemiology,* 1973, 98:463-445.

Ross, M. Suicide among physicians. *Diseases of the Nervous System,* 1973, 34:145-150.

Q: *Is anorexia nervosa a type of suicidal behavior?*

A: In anorexia nervosa, a person loses her appetite and restricts food intake to the point of emaciation. Psychologists today distinguish severe dieting (anorexia) from binge eating followed by the induction of diarrhea or vomiting (bulimia).

Anorexia nervosa overwhelmingly affects adolescent girls. About 90 percent of anorectics are women, and the onset is typically between the ages of twelve and eighteen. Most psychologists consider a weight loss of 25 percent as indicative of anorexia. Despite the fact that anorectics are often emaciated, they continue to have a strong fear of gaining weight and insist that they are still too fat.

There are many psychological theories of what causes people to become anorectics, including the fear of assuming an adult sexual role and power struggles with domineering parents.

Psychoanalysts such as Karl Menninger would see anorexia as a form of self-destructive behavior (chronic suicide), in which the person is impairing her life and hastening her death by her disturbed eating behavior.

Tolstrup, et al. (1985) conducted a follow-up study on 151 cases of anorexia. When traced, the patients' average age was 31; the average follow-up period was about 12 years (since they were first seen at the clinic).

Nine of the 151 patients had died, a very high mortality rate for young adolescents. Six of the dead were clearly suicides, two were dead from malnutrition and one death was considered a possible suicide. Thus, assuming that the results of this follow-up study are replicated by other investigators, it is clear that suicidal behavior is extremely common in anorectics, which clearly supports the conceptualization of anorexia as a severely self-destructive behavior.

Reference

Tolstrup, K., Brinch, M., Isager, T., Nielsen, S., Nystrup, J., Severin, B., and Olesen, N. S. Long-term outcome of 151 cases of anorexia nervosa. *Acta Psychiatrica Scandinavia,* 1985, 71:380-387.

Q: *Why does sexual abuse seem to increase the risk of suicide?*

A: Recent studies have found that experiences of sexual abuse in childhood increase the risk of suicide in later life. For example, Briere and Runtz (1986) have reported that 133 women (68%) referred to a crisis clinic had experienced sexual abuse as children, and only 62 had not. The typical victim was first sexually abused at the age of eight and the abuse ended at the age of 14. The mean number of assailants per victim was 1.8. Oral intercourse or anal/vaginal penetration occured in 77 percent of the victims. The abuse was incestuous for 61 percent of the victims, and over half (56%) of the sexual abuse victims also reported other physical abuse.

Of the women who had been sexually abused, 55 percent attempted suicide later in life, as compared to only 23 percent of those who had not been abused. The number of attempts at suicide was greater if the victim had experienced both sexual and physical abuse and if the abuse had included intercourse.

Briere and Runtz suggested that sexual abuse leads to impaired self-esteem and self-blame. Irrationally, the victim of sexual abuse often comes to see herself as responsible for precipitating the abuse, and as deserving it. This self-blame, combined with low self-esteem, increases the risk of self-destructiveness.

Sexual abuse also makes the victim feel powerless. Learned helplessness is a psychological phenomenon in which victims are hurt in situations where avoidance is not possible; and depression may sometimes result from learned helplessness. Thus, the powerless feeling experienced by victims of sexual abuse may increase the severity of their depression. The suicidal behavior may also represent an attempt to restore power to a person who feels powerless.

Finally, sexual abuse in childhood may hinder the victim

when she tries to establish relationships later in life. This increases the likelihood of interpersonal conflict and produces feelings of isolation and alienation when relationships break up.

It is therefore crucial that counselors of suicidal women explore the possibility that they were victims of sexual abuse. It would be difficult to help the women resolve their problems and end the suicidal crisis unless the unresolved feelings from the sexual abuse were brought out and discussed.

Reference

Briere, J., and Runtz, M. Suicidal thoughts and behaviours in former sexual abuse victims. *Canadian Journal of Behavioural Science,* 1986, 18:413-423.

Q: *How do suicide rates vary with age?*

A: In the United States, the effect of age on suicide rates varies for men and women. For men, the suicide rate rises steadily with age. For women the suicide rate peaks in middle age. The following are the suicide rates by age per 100,000 per year for 1980:

Age	Men	Women
5–14	0.7	0.2
15–24	20.2	4.3
25–34	24.8	7.0
35–44	22.3	8.4
45–54	23.0	9.4
55–64	24.4	8.4
65–74	30.2	6.5
75+	43.5	5.4

Note that the suicide rate for men is highest for those 75 and older. (In recent years, the rising suicide rate in youth has introduced a minor secondary peak.) For women, the suicide rates peak at age 45–55, and then begins to fall in later years.

One explanation for this disparity is that there are many more elderly women living than elderly men, and it may be that this fact and better social skills make women more successful at forming social networks of friends to help them construct a satisfactory life in old age.

Fuse (1980) described three patterns for the variation of suicide rates with age:

Pattern A: Suicide rates peak in old age.
Pattern B: Suicide rates peak in middle age.
Pattern C: Suicide rates peak in youth with
a minor peak in old age.

Lester (1982) examined the relation of suicide rates to age in nations of the world (according to their level of economic development). In all nations, men followed Pattern A, having the highest suicide rates in old age. Women, however, followed Pattern B in the most economically developed nations, Pattern A in the poorer nations, and Pattern C in the poorest nations.

The variation of suicide rates with age appears to change over time and probably will change more in future years.

References

Fuse, T. To be or not to be. *Stress,* 1980, 1(3):18-25.
Lester, D. The distribution of sex and age among completed suicides. *International Journal of Social Psychiatry,* 1982, 28:256-260.

Q: Is suicide more common in homosexuals?

A: Although not much research has been conducted on this issue, Saunders and Valente (1987) recently reviewed available information and concluded that the rate of attempted suicide was higher in gay men and lesbians than in heterosexuals. There is even less evidence available whether this is also true for completed suicide, but it is likely that rates of completed suicide are also higher in homosexuals.

Leaving aside the problem of the high incidence of AIDS among gay people, Saunders and Valente pointed out that homosexuals have a higher incidence of alcohol and drug abuse than heterosexuals and more disruptions and conflicts in their social ties. (Their intimate relationships are often less stable and they are frequently in conflict with relatives over their sexual life style.) These factors may be responsible for the increase in their suicidal behavior.

In addition, the act of coming out (admitting to yourself and to others that you are gay) is very stressful, and many homosexuals experience psychiatric problems, including suicidal thoughts, during this period (Schneider, et al., 1985). These problems may influence suicidal behavior more than the personal characteristics of homosexuals. In fact, Rich, et al. (1986) collected information on a sample of completed suicides in San Diego and found few differences in the personal and social characteristics of the homosexuals and heterosexuals in the sample.

References

Rich, C. L., Fowler, R. C., Young, D., and Blenkush, M. San Diego suicide study. *Suicide and Life-Threatening Behavior,* 1986, 16:448-457.

Saunders, J. M., and Valente, S. M. Suicide risk among gay men and lesbians. *Death Studies,* 1987, 11:1-23.

Schneider, S. G., Farberow, N. L. and Kruks, G. N. Suicidal behavior in adolescent and young adult gay men. In R. I. Yufit (Ed.) *Proceedings of the Twentieth Annual Conference.* Denver: American Association of Suicidology, 1987, 132-134.

Q: *Are suicide rates higher among the widowed and divorced?*

A: It is generally true that suicide rates are highest in those who are widowed and divorced and lowest in those who are married. In the United States in 1959 for those aged 35 to 44 (Dublin, 1963), the suicide rates per 100,000 per year were as follows:

	Males	Females
Single	29.8	9.4
Married	16.7	5.9
Widowed	81.7	10.2
Divorced	112.6	24.4

The high suicide rates in the widowed may be a direct result of the sadness and depression of bereavement. Although less likely, it may also be that those who are depressed and suicidally inclined are less likely to remarry.

The even higher suicide rate among the divorced may be because each partner played a role in precipitating the loss; thus, there is the potential on both sides for anger toward the partner as well as self-blame. Since suicide can be motivated in part, not only by the desire to escape from pain, but also by the desire to aggress against the self and others, the likelihood of suicide may well be higher in the divorced.

The higher suicide rate of those who are single over those who are married is not found among those who marry very young (in their teens). On the contrary, in this latter group some reports indicate a higher suicide rate among the married. It seems that the stresses of marriage at an early age increase the likelihood of suicide.

Gove (1972) noted that marriage appears to be associated with a lower suicide rate than being single. However, he showed that his benefit was greater for men than for women. Single males were 97 percent more likely to commit suicide than married men, whereas single women were only 47 percent more likely to commit suicide than married women. He argued that marriage was more advantageous to men than to women, and he presented data on rates of psychiatric illness to support this conclusion.

Interestingly, there has been very little research conducted on whether the presence of children reduces the suicide rate of married people even further. Data from the last century, however, do suggest that married people with children have the lowest suicide rates of all (Dublin and Bunzel, 1933).

References

Dublin, L. I. *Suicide.* New York: Ronald, 1963.
Dublin, L. I., and Bunzel, B. *To be or not to be.* New York: Smith and Hass, 1933.
Gove, W. Sex, marital status and suicide. *Journal of Health and Social Behavior,* 1972, 13:204-213.

Q: Can a child commit suicide?

A: Official government health statistics do not count any deaths of children younger than fourteen years of age as suicide; therefore, officially, children cannot commit suicide.

If we adopt a narrow definition of suicide, a person committing suicide must have a mature concept of death and must intentionally seek to die. This concept is thought to be beyond the capacity of children under 14 years. Children often view death as a kind of sleep, and in this sense they think that people can die and then come back to life again. Some children personify death, seeing it as a person who takes you away. If such children die because of some action that they take, such as running out into traffic, we cannot be sure that they had a mature concept of death and were seeking to die.

However, we need not subscribe to such a narrow definition of suicide. These criteria of suicide behavior may be too restricted. Furthermore, when we listen to self-destructive children, it is not unusual to hear statements similar to those made by people with a mature concept of death. They may threaten to kill themselves or wish that they were dead. Thus, if we focus on observable behaviors, it seems possible for children to commit suicide. Only if we focus on the concepts and desires in the mind do we have doubts.

Reference

Pfeffer, C. *The suicidal child.* New York: Guilford, 1986.

Q: Can suicide be an impulsive act?

A: It has often been suggested that impulsivity is characteristic of those who attempt or complete suicide, especially younger people. Corder, et al. (1974) found that adolescent suicide attempters were more impulsive and more active in general than nonsuicidal adolescents. Lester (1967) noted that students who reported having attempted or threatened suicide were more irritable than nonsuicidal students (questions about impulsivity were included in the measure of irritability).

Kessel (1967) found that about two-thirds of a group of self-poisoners were impulsive. Five minutes before the act, the idea of taking poison had not even been in their mind. (This does not mean that they had never considered suicide before.) In this study, impulsivity was less common in the elderly: it was not related to sex, alcoholism, intoxication, or the choice of method for suicide. The impulsive acts were, however, less lethal.

Williams, et al. (1977) compared impulsive attempters (who had acted within five minutes of thinking about suicide) with nonimpulsive attempters and found no difference in age, sex, or alcoholic intoxication. The impulsive attempters were more likely to have made prior suicide attempts, had the means for suicide more readily available, and had ingested greater dosages of the drug used for suicide.

Thus, it appears that a good proportion of suicide attempters are impulsive. They differ from non-impulsive attempters in that they tend to be repeaters and to have the means for suicide readily available. However, research results conflict on whether impulsive attempters are younger and use more lethal methods.

References

Corder, B., Shorr, W., and Corder, R. A study of social and psychological characteristics of adolescent suicide attempters in an urban disadvantaged area. *Adolescence,* 1974, 9:1-16.

Kessel, N. Self-poisoning. In E. S. Shneidman (Ed). *Essays in self-destruction.* New York: Science House, 1967, 345-372.

Lester, D. Suicide as an aggressive act. *Journal of Psychology,* 1967, 66:47-50.

Williams, C., Sale, I., and Wagnell, A. Correlates of impulsive suicidal behavior. *New Zealand Medical Journal,* 1977, 85:323-325.

Q: *Do suicidal and nonsuicidal people think in similar ways?*

A: For those who have never seriously considered suicide, the thought processes of suicidal people probably seem irrational; it is appropriate to ask how much is known about the ways in which suicidal people think.

To explore this issue Neuringer has given a variety of problem-solving tasks to suicidal and nonsuicidal patients. When asked to evaluate various concepts, using rating scales, suicidal patients tended to make more extreme ratings (such as *very* good or *very* bad) than other patients (Neuringer, 1988). Furthermore, on various tests of rigid thinking, suicidal patients tended to show greater rigidity than nonsuicidal patients.

Thus it is possible that, when faced with a real-life problem, suicidal people tend to be rigid and, therefore, identify fewer alternative solutions. They may also tend to think more dichotomously, leading them to exaggerate their evaluations of their conditions and limit the solutions that they can identify. (For example, a person may decide that his life is *horrible* and death is the *only* sensible solution to his problems.)

Some tentative evidence suggests that suicidal people to tend to externalize blame for their misfortunes more often than do nonsuicidal people (Lester, 1983). Psychologists generally view this orientation (that someone or something else caused the problem) as unhealthy and less likely to lead to appropriate problem-solving than holding oneself responsible for one's situation.

For these reasons, many of the psychotherapeutic approaches now used for counseling suicidal people focus on changing the thinking patterns just mentioned (Patsiokas and Clum, 1985).

References

Lester, D. *Why people kill themselves.* Springfield: Thomas, 1983.
Neuringer, C. The thinking process in suicidal women. In D. Lester
(Ed.) *Why women kill themselves.* Springfield: Thomas, 1988.
Patsiokas, A. T., and Clum, G. A. Effects of psychotherapeutic
strategies in the treatment of suicide attempters. *Psycho-
therapy,* 1985, 22:281-290.

Q: Can suicide be a manipulative act?

A: Lester (1987) has pointed out that self-injurious behaviors are often rewarded by others. It may be that family and friends pay more attention to a person who has injured himself. Even if the attention also involves punishment, the person may still find it rewarding, particularly if the previous attitude of others was to ignore him. In studies of children self-injurious behavior was less common when the child was alone than when he was with a parent.

Suicidal behavior has often been considered a manipulative act. Indeed, Farberow and Shneidman's (1961) classic book on attempted suicide was entitled *The Cry for Help* in order to draw attention to the desire of attempted suicides to manipulate others through the suicidal act.

Sifneos (1966) studied a group of attempted suicides and was struck by the manipulative aspects of their behavior. He judged 66 percent to have used their suicidal attempts to control others (for example, to prevent a spouse from leaving them). Sifneos noted that the majority of the suicide attempters were satisfied with the results of their manipulative behavior and were not motivated to receive psychotherapy. Anxiety was often lacking, and they appeared to be apathetic and fatalistic. They seemed to be more introspective and self-centered; they had few but rather intense relationships; they had difficulty expressing emotions; they exaggerated expectations of themselves; and they internalized problems.

References

Farberow, N. L., and Shneidman, E. S. (Eds.) *The cry for help.* New York: McGraw-Hill, 1961.

Lester, D. *Suicide as a learned behavior.* Springfield: Thomas, 1987.

Sifneos, P. Manipulative suicide. *Psychiatric Quarterly,* 1966, 40:525-537.

Q: *Does the state of the national economy have an impact on suicide rates?*

A: It has been said that suicide was quite common during the Great Depression in the 1930s in the United States. MacMahon, et al. (1963) noted that the rise in the suicide rate was apparent only for males, especially older males. Furthermore, the suicide rate appeared to be more affected by general economic conditions rather than specific, dramatic events such as the stock market crash.

These observations raise the question of how suicide rates relate to the national economy. Henry and Short (1954) found a negative correlation between the suicide rate and economic prosperity in the United States. In other words, suicide rates rose during times of business depression and fell during times of prosperity. This association was stronger for males, for those who were married, and for those with higher incomes. Hamermesh and Soss (1974) confirmed this for the post-World War II period in a study of male suicide rates, but only for those above 34 years of age.

In contrast, studies comparing different nations find suicide rates to be actually higher in more prosperous nations than in poorer countries (Stack, 1979). This means that results from analyses of suicide rates and the economy over time within a single country (such as the United States) seem to produce very different conclusions from comparative studies of several nations.

References

Hamermesh, D. S., and Soss, N. M. An economic theory of suicide. *Journal of Political Economy,* 1974, 82:83-98.

Henry, A. F., and Short, J. F. *Suicide and homicide.* New York: Free Press, 1954.

MacMahon, B., Johnson, S., and Pugh, T. Relation of suicide rates to social conditions. *Public Health Reports,* 1963, 78:285-293.

Stack, S. Suicide. *Social Forces,* 1978, 57:644-653.

Q: *How does socioeconomic class affect the suicide rate?*

A: Surprisingly, suicide rates by social class have not shown a consistent pattern. In England and Wales, the classes are defined as follows:

Class 1	professions/highest ranks of business
Class 2	entrepreneurs/managers/retail traders/ clerks/teachers/farm owners
Class 3	skilled workers
Class 4	agricultural laborers
Class 5	unskilled workers

Dublin (1963) reported the relative suicide rate for men aged 20 to 64 in 1949-1953 at 140 per 100,000 for Class 1, 113 for Class 2, 89 for Class 3, 92 for Class 4, and 117 for Class 5. Thus, it appears that the highest and lowest classes have higher suicide rates, while the middle classes have lower suicide rates.

The evidence from other countries has been contradictory. In New Zealand Porterfield and Gibbs (1960) found higher suicide rates in the upper social classes, whereas in the United States, Tuckman, et al. (1964) found higher suicide rates in those with lower occupational status. More recently, Labovitz and Hagedorn (1971) found no association between suicide rates and the prestigiousness of occupations in the U.S.

In the New Zealand study, it was found that those who completed suicide tended to fall in social class during their lifetime rather than rise. Breed (1963), in the U.S., found that suicides were more likely to have experienced downward mobility during their own lives and downward mobility as compared to their parents.

In an interesting study, Shneidman and Farberow (1960) compared the suicide notes of people living in different socioeconomic areas in Los Angeles County. Those living in apartments in the most advantaged areas made many references to ill-health and were concerned with the absolution of others. Those living in apartments in the least advantaged areas gave few reasons for their suicide and communicated little emotion or affection. This implies that regardless of the rates of suicide, the reasons for suicide may differ in those of different social classes.

References

Breed, W. Occupational mobility and suicide among white males. *American Sociological Review,* 1963, 28:179-188.

Dublin, L. I. *Suicide.* New York: Ronald, 1963.

Labovitz, S., and Hagedorn, R. An analysis of suicide rates among occupational categories. *Sociological Inquiry,* 1971, 41:67-72.

Porterfield, A. L., and Gibbs, J. P. Occupational prestige and social mobility of suicides in New Zealand. *American Journal of Sociology,* 1960, 66:147-152.

Shneidman, E. S., and Farberow, N. L. A socio-psychological investigation of suicide. In H. P. David and J. C. Brengelmann (Eds.) *Perspectives on personality research.* New York: Springer, 1960, 270-293.

Tuckman, J., Youngman, W. F., and Kreizman, G. Occupation and suicide. *Industrial Medicine and Surgery,* 1964, 33:818-820.

Q: *Are suicide rates influenced by unemployment rates?*

A: Platt (1986) has noted that at least 20 studies have been published which include information about the incidence of unemployment in samples of attempted suicides. The general conclusion of these studies is that attempted suicide is far more common among the unemployed than the employed. For example, in 1982 in Oxford, England, the attempted suicide rate among unemployed men was 708 per 100,000 per year compared to only 46 among employed men. In Edinburgh in 1982 the rates were 1345 and 114, respectively.

The rate of attempted suicide appears to increase as the duration of unemployment lengthens. Also the relatively higher rate of attempted suicide among the unemployed was greater in the higher social classes. Unemployed attempters were more depressed and hopeless than employed attempters.

Unemployed men who attempted suicide were more likely than employed attempted suicides to have received psychiatric treatment in the past, to have been diagnosed as an alcohol or drug abuser, to have made prior attempts at suicide, to be unmarried, to have experienced early separation from his mother, and to have a criminal record. These differences suggest that there are several childhood and personal characteristics that predispose certain men to both unemployment and suicidal behavior. It is important that future studies identify the time sequence in these behaviors and determine, for example, whether the alcoholism predates the unemployment, or the unemployment predates the alcoholism.

Platt (1984) also found that there were significantly more unemployment, job instability, and occupational problems among completed suicides. Despite this association, Platt argued that unemployment in its own right may not directly lead to increased rates of completed suicide, but it may be part of a causal chain (as with attempted suicides). He rejected the possibility that unemployment leads to both psychiatric

71

illness and suicide, and preferred the possibility that psychiatric illness leads to both unemployment and suicide, with unemployment adding a small amount of risk of suicide.

References

Platt, S. Unemployment and suicidal behavior. *Social Science and Medicine,* 1984, 19:93-115.
Platt, S. Parasuicide and unemployment. *British Journal of Psychiatry,* 1986, 149:401-405.

Q: *Are there epidemics of suicide?*

A: It certainly appears from the newspapers that epidemics of suicide exist. A report of one suicide is sometimes followed by reports of similar suicides in the next few days. However, this is often simply a result of newspapers suddenly paying attention to suicides and later losing interest.

For example, suicide is very common at certain locales, such as the Golden Gate Bridge in San Francisco and Niagara Falls. However, suicides at these locales tend to occur at a steady rate, month after month, year after year, and no clustering is aparent (Kirch and Lester, 1986).

On the other hand, there is evidence that after certain instances of suicide, there is an increase in other suicides, often "copy-cat suicides," in the next few days or weeks. Phillips (1974) has shown that famous suicides, such as Marilyn Monroe's, lead to an increase in the number of suicides in the following week. Coleman (1987) has demonstrated that some teenage suicides appear to precipitate similar suicides in the community, which often use the same method and location for suicide.

Also, clusters of attempted suicides have been documented in military bases (Hankoff, 1961) and hospitals (Crawford and Willis, 1966).

References

Coleman, L. *Suicide clusters.* Boston, Faber and Faber, 1987.

Crawford, J., and Willis, J. Double suicide in psychiatric hospital patients. *British Journal of Psychiatry,* 1966, 112:1231-1235.

Hankoff, L. An epidemic of attempted suicide, *Comprehensive Psychiatry,* 1861, 2:294-298.

Kirch, M., and Lester, D. Suicides from the Golden Gate Bridge. *Psychological Reports,* 1986, 59:1314.

Phillips, D. The influences of suggestion on suicide. *American Sociological Review,* 1974, 39:340-354.

Q: Do police officers have a high suicide rate?

A: Suicide in police officers is of particular interest because police officers are of course equipped with the means to kill themselves efficiently, namely firearms. Is the possession of a lethal weapon associated with a higher suicide rate?

Interestingly, there is little data on suicide rates by occupation because many death certificates do not record the occupation of the deceased. However, several studies in diferent regions have reported a high rate of suicide in police officers (in Chicago, New York City, Tennessee and Wyoming), although other studies (e.g., in Los Angeles) have not confirmed these high rates (see Lester, 1978).

In one national study using data from 1950, Labovitz and Hagedorn (1971) found that police officers had the second highest suicide rate of 36 occupations. (British police officers, however, appear to have an average suicide rate [Heiman, 1975].)

In a study of just 12 police officers who committed suicide in Detroit, Danto (1978) found that eight used firearms and two used car exhaust. Interestingly, four of the police officers had murdered someone before committing suicide, including two wives and one ex-husband of a wife. Five of the officers had received a psychiatric evaluation, and four of these were diagnosed as psychotic. None of the officers were in their uniform at the time of death. Danto felt that the primary stress on these men was interpersonal, primarily from their marriages, not their jobs.

References

Danto, B. L. Police suicide. *Police Stress,* 1978, 1(1):32-40.
Heiman, M. Police suicides revisited. *Suicide,* 1975, 5:5-20.
Labovitz, S., and Hagedorn, R. An analysis of suicide rates among occupational categories. *Sociological Inquiry,* 1971, 41:6-72.
Lester, D. Suicide in police officers. *Police Chief,* 1978, 45(4):17.

Q: *Is it true that psychiatrists have a high suicide rate?*

A: A study more than 20 years ago by Blachly, et al. (1968) reported the suicide rate of doctors according to speciality. They found that overall, physicians had an average suicide rate, but that the rate did vary by specialty: psychiatrists had the highest suicide rate (61 per 100,000 per year) while pediatricians had the lowest rate (10).

Since Blachly's study, research has tended to support that fact that physicians in general have an average suicide rate (Lester, 1983). However, these more recent studies have not re-examined the variation in suicide rates by specialty. The conclusions about the high rate in psychiatrists has not been challenged.

Why should psychiatrists have a higher suicide rate than other physicians? Investigators have considered the type of stress experienced by all kinds of counselors (including psychologists, social workers, and psychiatrists) and speculate that these careers involve stressors that are especially likely to lead to suicide. Paradoxically, perhaps, other counselors such as social workers and clergymen have been found to have low suicide rates (Rose and Rosnow, 1973).

An alternative explanation has focused on whether different kinds of people are attracted to different specialities. Perhaps psychiatry attracts more people who have a greater propensity to psychiatric illness and suicide than do the other specialties.

Also, the higher suicide rate in psychiatrists may no longer be found in the 1980s. New studies are necessary to confirm or refute Blachly's report. Furthermore, the fact that psychiatrists had the highest suicide rate in Blachly's report confirmed the popular belief that psychiatrists and psychologists are often "crazy"; consequently, the findings have received wide publicity and were well accepted. However, lost in the publicity was the fact that ophthalmologists and otolaryngologists had the second highest suicide rate (55 per 100,000 per year), for reasons that are far more difficult to identify.

References

Blachly, P. H., Disher, W., and Roduner, G. Suicide by physicians. *Bulletin of Suicidology,* 1968, December, 1-18.
Lester, D. *Why people kill themselves.* Springfield: Thomas, 1983.
Rose, K., and Rosnow, I. Physicians who kill themselves. *Archives of General Psychiatry,* 1973, 29:800-805.

Q: *How common is suicide in black Americans?*

A: Suicide is much less common in black Americans than white Americans (whereas being a victim of homicide is much more common among blacks). For example, in 1980 the rates of death by suicide and homicide per 100,000 were as follows:

	Suicide	Homicide
White males	19.9	10.7
White females	5.9	3.2
Black males	10.3	65.7
Black females	2.2	13.5

(The homicide rates are for victims, but since most murders are intra-racial the rates are probably similar for murderers.)

Interestingly, this racial difference in suicide and homicide rates is also found in South Africa where the disparity in socioeconomic status between whites and blacks is even more pronounced (Lester, 1988); and in Zimbabwe where blacks now govern the country (Lester and Wilson, 1988).

In America, particular groups of blacks sometimes have high suicide rates. For example, Hendin (1969) noted that young black males in New York City had a high suicide rate in the 1960s, with jumping off buildings as a common method.

Henry and Short (1954) suggest that oppressed people are likely to have higher levels of anger and so be more assaultive, resulting in higher homicide rates. In contrast, oppressors would have higher levels of self-blame and so be more depressed, creating higher suicide rates. Data from blacks and whites in the USA support his hypothesis.

Studies comparing blacks and whites who attempt or complete suicide have revealed few differences of any interest. (For example, Breed [1970] found no differences in social class, family situation, or personal difficulties. The black suicides had experienced more trouble with authorities such as the police and landlords.) Thus, it is not at all certain that the motivation and causes of suicide in blacks differ from those in whites.

References

Breed, W. The negro and fatalistic suicide. *Pacific Sociological Review,* 1970, 13:156-162.

Hendin, H. *Black suicide.* New York: Basic Books, 1969.

Henry, A. F., and Short, J. F. *Suicide and homicide.* New York: Free Press, 1954.

Lester, D. Personal violence (suicide and homicide) in South Africa. *Acta Psychiatrica Scandinavia,* 1988, 78, in press.

Lester, D., and Wilson, C. T. Suicide in Zimbabwe. *Central African Journal of Medicine,* 1988, in press.

Q: *Does suicide become less common as the quality of life improves?*

A: Common sense suggests that suicide would be more common when life is bad. As life gets better and better, we should be less inclined to think about suicide and less likely to go ahead and actually kill ourselves.

But what do we mean by bad, and how can this be measured? A number of investigators have tried to use various social, economic, and climatic conditions to rate the quality of life in different geographic regions. When the ratings of the quality of life in the United States and other nations are compared to the suicide rates of these regions, we find that suicide is more common in regions where the quality of life is better (Lester, 1986).

Lester has explained this surprising result by using a theory proposed by Henry and Short (1954). Henry and Short argued that when people can blame their unhappiness and misfortunes on others, they become angry rather than depressed. However, when they have no external sources to blame for their distress, they will become depressed and full of self-blame, which increases their risk of suicide.

As the quality of life improves, then, there are fewer external sources to blame for distress. If a person has failed to achieve whatever he wanted to achieve, he has only himself to blame. Thus, suicide would become more common.

This concept can be illustrated by the "if only" phenomenon. There are many of us who say, "If only I had X, then life would be fine." Perhaps we obtain X (whatever it is, a spouse, a new job, a nice house, a new car) and find that we are still unhappy. A few people go on from X to Y to Z, always focusing on a new goal which will make them happy. What happens when they eventually realize that happiness comes from an internal state of mind and not from some external object? They may realize that unhappiness comes from within, and their depression may deepen unless they have resources to help them cope with this identity crisis.

Of course there are many aspects to the quality of life that cannot be measured. In some respects, the quality of the life of teenagers has improved tremendously over the last century. The present generation are affluent, well cared for, and can be idle if they choose. As their quality of life has improved, their suicide rates have increased accordingly. However, in less tangible ways, one could argue that teenagers today are subjected to stresses that are quite different from those of earlier generations (including decisions of whether to resist peer pressures for such behaviors as drug use and premarital sex; parents whose divorce and remarriage rates have increased greatly; and increased media focus on global concerns such as nuclear war and environmental pollution). Unfortunately these stresses are unmeasurable by most of the indices of the quality of life.

References

Henry, A. F., and Short, J. F. *Suicide and homicide.* New York: Free Press, 1954.

Lester, D. Suicide, homicide, and the quality of life. *Suicide and Life-Threatening Behavior,* 1986, 16:389-392.

Q: What methods are used most often for suicide?

A: In the United States the most common method for completing suicide is firearms. It has been by far the most common method for males for many years, and, in recent years, it has also become the most widely used method for females, replacing poisoning. The following data are from 1980, obtained from the *Vital Statistics of the United States.*

Method	Suicide Rate		Percent Using Each Method	
	Males	Females	Males	Females
Poisoning				
Solid & liquids	1.1	1.3	5.6%	26.1%
Gases & vapors	1.7	0.6	8.8%	11.7%
Hanging/strangulation/				
suffocation	3.0	0.6	15.3%	11.6%
Submersion	0.2	0.2	1.2%	2.9%
Firearms & explosives	12.8	2.1	64.0%	40.5%
Cutting & piercing				
instruments	0.3	0.1	1.5%	1.4%
Jumping from high places	0.4	0.2	2.2%	3.4%
Other methods	0.3	0.1	1.5%	2.3%

Poisoning by solid and liquid substances remains quite common for females (26.1%), but much less frequent for males (5.6%). Suicide by gases and vapors is primarily accomplished today by means of car exhaust, since domestic gas is now relatively non-toxic. Although mild attempts at suicide are often made by cutting wrists (and, less commonly, other parts of the body), the rate of completed suicide using cutting and piercing instruments is very low, indicating that this is a relatively non-lethal method.

The methods used for suicide vary considerably from country to country (Farmer and Rohde, 1980). For example, in most nations, firearms are not used as extensively as in the United States. People in underdeveloped countries commonly use pesticides and fertilizers for suicide (Berger, 1988), while those in urban settings in the Far East (such as Hong Kong and Singapore) more commonly jump from high buildings.

References

Berger, L. R. Suicides and pesticides in Sri Lanka. *American Journal of Public Health,* 1988, 78:826-828.

Farmer, R., and Rohde, J. Effect of availability and acceptability of lethal instruments on suicide mortality. *Acta Psychiatrica Scandinavia,* 1980, 62:436-446.

Q: *What is a suicidal gesture?*

A: Many people make token acts of committing suicide. They may, for example, cut lightly across their wrists with a razor blade, which causes bleeding, but is not likely to lead to death. Similarly, other individuals will swallow a handful of aspirin tablets in view of others, or notify someone immediately after swallowing them. Although it is possible for a person to kill himself by ingesting a large number of aspirin (if he can keep himself from vomiting), taking aspirin is a relatively non-lethal method of attempting suicide. The same can be said of trying to jump out of a window when others are in the room, or stringing up ropes or sheets while others are present to intervene.

These relatively non-lethal actions are called suicidal *gestures,* since the person who attempts them is really only communicating that he is upset and is thinking about suicide but is not planning to die as a result of his present actions. A suicidal gesture usually represents a cry for help.

Those who make gestures at suicide are not to be taken lightly. Although there have been no good follow-up studies to calculate the exact risk of suicide in these people, the suicide rate is certainly higher than the rate for those who have never attempted suicide. For example, the novelist Ernest Hemingway tried in the presence of his wife and friends to walk into the propellers of an airplane and to jump from the plane once it had taken off. Although these were gestures, he killed himself a few months later. Actress Marilyn Monroe took an overdose of barbiturates while her husband Arthur Miller was at home; several years later she died of a drug overdose.

Q: *Is wrist-cutting a seriously suicidal act?*

A: It is not unusual for distraught people to cut or slash their wrists. This behavior is most common in female teenagers, particularly those who are psychiatrically disturbed. In more of these cases, the wrist-cutting is labelled "delicate" (as opposed to "coarse").

Delicate wrist-cutting is typically on the arms, although it may also include the legs or face. Usually the cuts are superficial and run from side to side (rather than along the length of the arm), and therefore rarely serious or life-threatening. Often the act is compulsive, with inner tension building up until the person feels compelled to cut, whereupon the tension seems to ebb as the blood begins to flow. Those who have cut themselves report little or no pain from the cutting (Graff and Mallin, 1967). Wrist-cutting may be attempted time after time.

Many writers on the subject minimize the suicidal intent of wrist-cutters. However, no study has ever followed up teenage wrist-cutters to determine the likelihood of their dying from suicide. Since wrist-cutting is a mildly self-destructive act, it would not be surprising to find that the risk of eventual suicide among these people is greater than average.

Similarly, the risk of suicide in those who use other forms of self-mutilation (Lester, 1972), such as head-banging, hair pulling, and the like, has never been studied, but may well be higher than average. Menninger (1938) was convinced of the pervasiveness of a self-destructive impulse in humans and saw self-mutilation as a manifestation of this drive, albeit in a milder form than is shown in overt acts of suicide.

References

Graff, H., and Mallin, R. The syndrome of the wrist-cutter. *American Journal of Psychiatry,* 1967, 124:36-42.

Lester, D. Self-mutilating behavior. *Psychological Bulletin,* 1972, 78:119-128.

Menninger, K. *Man against himself.* New York: Harcourt, Brace and World, 1938.

Q: *Are there subtle, indirect ways of killing yourself?*

A: There are many ways of committing suicide that often get misclassified, usually under the guise of accidents. It has long been suspected, for example, that many single car crashes are in fact suicides. However, Tabachnick (1973) found many differences between those who shot themselves and those who died in single car crashes. Although both groups had been drinking prior to their death equally often, and both were impulsive and concerned with performance, the accident cases had not experienced recent loss as often as the suicides, and had more often recently assumed positions of greater responsibility. In response to criticism, the accident cases had become angry while the gunshot suicides had become more depressed. Tabachnick concluded that the two groups were composed of different types of people, but the variation may mean simply that different types of people choose different methods for suicide.

There are many other methods for covertly committing suicide. For instance, diabetics may be lax in taking their insulin or in adhering to their diet; patients with other medical disorders can foster their own deaths in analogous ways. In *The Many Faces of Suicide,* Farberow (1980) discusses this form of suicidal behavior in detail.

Finally, many behavior patterns, such as alcoholism and drug abuse, can be seen as suicidal behaviors, although these behaviors differ from those first cited, in that the substance abuser may not necessarily have any conscious suicidal intent.

References

Farberow, N. L. *The many faces of suicide.* New York: McGraw-Hill, 1980.
Tabachnick, N. *Accident or suicide.* Springfield: Thomas, 1973.

Q: Are alcohol and drug addiction forms of suicide?

A: Mental health professionals vary widely in their perception of the suicidal impulse. Some hold a very narrow, strict view of the concept: suicide implies that a person understands the nature of death and consciously chooses death over life. Others, however, view suicide in broader terms and prefer to talk of the self-destructive impulse, which may operate consciously and unconsciously, with manifestations of this impulse in many types of behavior.

Menninger (1938), for example, noted that some people destory parts of their body. In mythology, when Oedipus, king of Thebes, discovered he had unwittingly murdered his father and married his mother, he blinded himself. Menninger documented less dramatic but similar cases in which people "accidentally" lost an arm or some other body part, often when feeling guilty over past misdeeds or when seriously depressed. Menninger felt that these individuals were behaving quite adaptively. Rather than destroying themselves completely in the act of suicide, they focused the self-destructive impulse on one part of the body, enabling the vital parts to survive. Menninger called this behavior *focal suicide* (the self-destructive impulse is focused on one part of the body).

Similarly, Menninger viewed long-term, chronic maladaptive behaviors that are deleterious to health as suicidal. Thus, the drug addict and the alcoholic are destroying themselves slowly, relentlessly decreasing their life expectancy. The heavy cigarette smoker, the homosexual who persists in engaging in casual anal sex with strangers, and the overweight person who continues to overeat are all increasing the risk of an early demise. Menninger called this behavior *chronic suicide*.

Reference

Menninger, K. *Man against himself.* New York: Harcourt, Brace, 1938.

Q: *Do alcoholics and drug addicts have high rates of suicide?*

A: Many believe that alcoholism and drug abuse should be viewed as forms of chronic suicide in which the person kills himself slowly over a long period of time. However, there is good evidence that alcoholics and drug abusers also have high rates of actual suicide.

Estimates of the incidence of attempted suicide among alcoholics range from 13 to 46 percent, and estimates of the incidence of completed suicide range from 7 to 21 percent (Rushing, 1968). It has been suggested that suicide is less common in the early stages of alcoholism (Robins and Murphy, 1965). A study of alcoholics who died from suicide and those who died from cirrhosis of the liver found that the suicidal group was more often diagnosed as psychiatrically disturbed. Also, they were more likely to be white, married, and employed, but did not differ in age, sex, or education (Haberman, 1979).

How can we account for the association of suicide and alcoholism? It is possible that both suicide and alcoholism are expressions of a common underlying factor—social disorganization or an oral personality, for example (Rushing, 1969). Alternatively, alcoholism may have a direct causal effect on suicidal behavior. Perhaps alcoholism causes physiological, personal, or social changes that increase the likelihood of sucide.

High rates of attempted suicide have also been reported in drug addicts (Saxon, et al., 1978). Completed suicide is also common in drug addicts, but suicide in drug addicts is difficult to distinguish from accidental overdoses of an abused drug, and therefore the suicide rate itself is uncertain.

References

Haberman, P. Cause of death in alcoholics. *Proceedings of the 10th International Congress on Suicide Prevention.* Ottawa: IASP, 1979, 108-115.

Rushing, W. Alcoholism and suicide rates by status set and occupation. *Quarterly Journal of Studies In Alcohol,* 1968, 29:399-412.

Rushing, W. Suicide and the interaction of alcoholism (liver cirrhosis) with the social situation. *Quarterly Journal of Studies in Alcohol,* 1969, 30:93-103.

Robins, E., and Murphy, G. E. The physician's role in the prevention of suicide. In L. Yochelson (Eds.) *Symposium on suicide.* Washington, DC: George Washington University Press, 1965, 84-91.

Saxon, S., Kuncel, E., and Aldrich, S. Drug abuse and suicide. *American Journal of Drug and Alcohol Abuse,* 1978, 5:485-495.

Q: *Can suicide be an act of anger or aggression?*

A: Menninger (1938) classified the motives for suicide into three broad categories: to die (or to escape from pain or psychological suffering); to be killed (to punish oneself for real or imagined bad deeds); and to kill (to aggress against others). This last motive clearly recognizes the possibility that anger can indeed be expressed through a suicidal act.

Sometimes the anger is expressed directly in a suicide note:

> *Mary,*
> *I hope you're satisfied.*
> *Bill* (Jacobs, 1967, p. 69)

> *Bill,*
> *I do hope you'll suffer more than I have done.*
> *I wish you'll die in a beer joint.*
> (Wagner, 1960, p. 63)

In other words, by committing suicide a person hopes to make others suffer and expects the survivor to feel guilt and shame. Indeed, survivors often do feel guilt for not responding in a way they feel may have been more appropriate. In fact, people often feel more negative emotion toward the survivors of suicides than they do toward the survivors of those dying natural deaths.

Suicides may also express anger through the method and location of the suicide. Those angry at their job may kill themselves at work. Those angry at loved ones may kill themselves in a horribly disfiguring manner, knowing that the loved ones will discover them.

Suicides are also found to be angry individuals. Suicidal patients are often more aggressive than other patients in a psychiatric hospital, and psychological tests find high levels of anger in suicidal people (Lester, 1987).

Thus, suicidal individuals are very likely to have high levels of anger and may seek to express this anger through the suicidal act.

References

Jacobs, J. A phenomenological study of suicide notes. *Social Problems,* 1967, 15, 60-72.

Lester, D. Murder and suicide: are they polar opposites? *Behavioral Sciences & The Law,* 1987, 5, 49-60.

Menninger, K. *Man against himself.* New York: Harcourt, Brace & World, 1938.

Wagner, F. F. Suicide notes. *Danish Medical Bulletin,* 1960, 7, 62-64.

Q: *Are suicide pacts common?*

A: Suicide pacts usually involve two individuals, both psychologically disturbed, who become entwined in a pathological relationship that encourages both to consider suicide when one of the two (or both) suffers some form of stress. Less often, suicide pacts involve one suicidal individual who persuades or forces a partner to die at the same time.

Suicide pacts are not very common. In a study in Dade County, Florida, Fishbain and Aldrich (1985) found 40 victims of suicide pacts out of 5895 suicides (only 0.7 percent). In Japan, only two percent of all suicide victims were involved in suicide pacts. However, suicide pacts attract a great deal of newspaper publicity, especially when the victims are famous. For example, Arthur Koestler, novelist and writer, committed suicide in a pact with his wife in 1983 (Goldney, 1986). The public's fascination with suicide pacts tends to exaggerate the incidence of these relatively uncommon events.

In Great Britain and America, most of the participants of suicide pacts appear to be spouses (Cohen, 1964; Fishbain, et al., 1984). In Japan, the majority are lovers (Ohara and Reynolds, 1970).

In the American study (Fishbain, et al., 1984), the people in suicide pacts more frequently included unemployed males, older individuals whose children had grown up and moved away, and those with themes of guilt and depression in their suicide notes. When the participants in the pact were lovers, there was less often a history of depression.

References

Cohen, J. *Behavior in uncertainty and its social consequences.* New York: Basic Books, 1964.

Fishbain, D. A. and Aldrich, T. E. Suicide pacts. *Journal of Clinical Psychiatry,* 1985, 46:11-15.

Fishbain, D. A., D'Achille, L., Barsky, S., and Aldrich, T. A controlled study of suicidal pacts. *Journal of Clinical Psychiatry,* 1984, 45:154-157.

Goldney, R. D. Arthur Koestler: was his suicide rational? *Crisis,* 1986, 7:33-38.

Ohara, K., and Renolds, D. Love-act suicides. *Omega,* 1970, 1:159-166.

Q: *Can you kill yourself by getting someone else to murder you?*

A: At first, this might seem like an odd question. Suicide, most of us would presume, is certainly very different from murder. Yet in a classic study of murder in Philadelphia, Wolfgang (1958) noted that many victims of murder seemed to act in such a way as to provoke their own murder: perhaps the victim had picked the fight in the first place or had goaded the eventual murderer into assaulting him.

For example, a drunken husband was beating his wife in the kitchen, gave her a knife and dared her to use it on him. She told him that if he hit her one more time, she would use the knife, whereupon he struck her, and she, in turn, stabbed him.

Wolfgang called this behavior victim-precipitated homicide, a murder in which the victim plays some role in precipitating his or her own murder. He found that 26 percent of the murders he studied in Philadelphia were in part victim-precipitated. This is consistent with the fact that murderers and their victims often have quite similar social characteristics and criminal histories, and are drunk at the time of the murder.

Wolfgang found that the victims of victim-precipitated homicide were more likely to be male, lower class, black, and more likely to have criminal records. They were more likely to have been drinking, and more likely to have been murdered by their spouses (particularly husbands murdered by wives). Interestingly, Wolfgang noted that the murderers in cases of victim-precipitated murder were less likely to commit suicide after the murder, possibly because they felt less guilty if the victim played a role in precipitating his or her own death.

In line with these ideas, some opponents of the death penalty have argued that the existence of a death penalty may induce suicidal people to commit murder in order to die by execution, a form of victim-precipitated murder in which the government kills the victim (Lester, 1987).

References

Lester, D. *The death penalty.* Springfield: Thomas, 1987.
Wolfgang, M. E. *Patterns of criminal homicide.* Philadelphia: University of Pennsylvania Press, 1958.

Q: Can a person cause someone else to commit suicide?

A: At one time or another, most of us have harbored hostile wishes toward others, even our loved ones. We think and sometimes say things like, "If it weren't for you, I could have done better. " Or we daydream about how our lives might be if the person were to die. For most of us, these thoughts and desires are rare and fleeting, but for some people, the wishes are strong. Although the desires may not be expressed consciously, the target person may nevertheless pick them up, consciously or unconsciously. These hostile thoughts may in turn influence the recipient to consider suicide. Meerloo (1962) called this behavior *psychic homicide;* in effect, it means that one person's hostility has indirectly caused another to kill himself.

For example, Meerloo described an engineer with a harsh, domineering and alcoholic father who gave his father a bottle of barbiturates to help "cure" his alcohol addiction. Two days later, the father killed himself with an overdose of alcohol and barbiturtes. The engineer could not admit that he had wanted his father to kill himself.

Richman (1986) has described even clearer instances of this type of behavior in which the hostile desires toward the suicidal person were more overtly expressed, to the point of stuffing pills into the suicide's mouth (which, of course, comes closer to murder).

One 17-year-old girl ran away with her boyfriend. When she came home, she became involved in a violent altercation with her parents, after which she swallowed her mother's tranquilizers. Later, in the hospital, the mother angrily told an interviewer that she would find her daughter's death easier to bear than the strain she was being put under. The daughter reported that her boyfriend was so ambivalent and hostile that she had told him, "If you want me to die, why don't you say so?" (Rosenbaum and Richman, 1970).

References

Meerloo, J. A. M. *Suicide and mass suicide.* New York: Grune and Stratton, 1962.

Richman, J. *Family therapy for suicidal people.* New York: Springer, 1986.

Rosenbaum, J., and Richman, J. Suicide. *American Journal of Psychiatry,* 1970, 126:1652-1655.

Q: *Do murderers often commit suicide after the crime?*

A: The frequency with which people kill themselves after murdering another person varies greatly from country to country. For example, in England and Wales about one-third of murderers commit suicide (West, 1966); by contrast, only about four percent of American murderers commit suicide (Wolfgang, 1958). The English murder rate is much lower than the American rate, but far fewer English murders involve crimes such as robbery where the victims are strangers.

This distinction is important because suicidal murderers are much more likely than other murderers to kill a close relative (such as a spouse, lover, or child). In America, husbands who murder their wives are more likely to commit suicide afterwards than wives who murder their husbands (perhaps because husbands are more violent and more often provoke their wives to murder, leaving the wives feeling less guilty).

Two groups of murderers have especially high rates of suicide. First, mothers who kill their children, especially for altruistic reasons, often commit suicide after the murder. Typically, these mothers are seriously depressed and their intention is to kill themselves. However, they think that their children will suffer so much after their suicide that they kill the children to prevent them from suffering (Resnick, 1969, 1970). Second, those who murder police officers also have a high incidence of suicide after the crime. Typically, these individuals are trapped, usually surrounded by police and exchanging gunfire. Often they are killed by the police during the shootout, but a high proportion of them actually take their own lives. Lester (1987) estimated the suicide rate for murderers who kill police officers as 3430 per 100,000 per year, as compared to the national suicide rate of 12.5.

References

Lester, D. Murder followed by suicide in those who murder police officers. *Psychological Reports,* 1987, 60:1130.

Resnick, P. Child murder by parents. *American Journal of Psychiatry,* 1969, 126:325-334.

Resnick, P. Murder of the newborn. *American Journal of Psychiatry,* 1970, 126:1414-1420.

West, D. *Murder followed by suicide.* Cambridge: Harvard University Press, 1966.

Wolfgang, M. E. *Patterns of criminal homicide.* Philadelphia: University of Pennsylvania Press, 1958.

Q: Why do so many prisoners kill themselves?

A: We often read in the newspaper that a prisoner has hanged himself. Often these prisoners are in local jails awaiting trial or sentencing. Paradoxically, suicide is most common among those arrested and charged with relatively minor crimes; the most common method used for suicide is hanging (since the methods for hanging are often available).

The relatively minor nature of the charges against these prisoners makes these suicides seem irrational. For example, Malcolm (1975) found that suicide in New York City jails was more common in nonaddicts, whites, males, and younger prisoners, and tended to occur more often during the first week of incarceration or after sixty days.

Suicide among convicted prisoners lodged in state prisons is also common, although not reported as often by newspapers. For prisoners in state institutions (where prisoners go after conviction) Lester (1982) computed a suicide rate for the period of 1978 to 1979 of 24.6 per 100,000 per year for men and 7.9 for women. These rates are only a little higher than the rates for the general population in 1980 of 18.6 for men and 5.5 for women. Because the rates for the general population include children, the suicide rates for prisoners are probably about the same as the incidence among adult Americans in general. However, high rates of suicide in prisoners has been noted in Belgium (Cosyns and Wilmotte, 1974), Canada (Burtch, 1979), and England (Topp, 1979).

In recent years there has been increasing public concern about suicides in those being held briefly in holding cells, jails, and prisons (as well as juveniles held temporarily in adult facilities). Staff members try to ensure that means for suicide are not readily available and carefully monitor prisoners who might be at high risk for suicide. Yet despite these precautions, prisoners still commit suicide. On death row, where prisoners are held awaiting execution, it might be thought that precautions against suicide would be especially thorough. However, Lester (1987) calculated the suicide rate to be 146.5, five or six times higher in death row residents than among prisoners in general.

References

Burtch, B. Prisoner suicide reconsidered. *International Journal of Law and Psychiatry,* 1979, 2, 407-413.

Cosyns, P., and Wilmotte, J. Suicidal behaviors in Belgian penitentiaries. *Proceedings of the 7th. International Congress for Suicide Prevention.* Amsterdam: Swets & Zeitlinger, 1974, 300-306.

Lester, D. Suicide and homicide in US prisons. *American Journal of Psychiatry,* 1982, 139:1527-1528.

Lester, D. *The death penalty.* Springfield: Thomas, 1987.

Malcolm, B. Today's problems in penology. *New York State Journal of Medicine,* 1975, 75:1812-1814.

Topp, D. Suicide in prison. *British Journal of Psychiatry,* 1979, 134:24-27.

$Q:$ *Are suicidal people risk-takers?*

$A:$ In many ways suicide can be seen as a gamble. The suicidal person is changing existences, exchanging the life he or she now has for an uncertain future. (Is there life after death?) For those with traditional religious beliefs, there is little assurance that life after suicide will be any less unpleasant than life on earth.

However, many potential suicides do not know for sure whether they will actually die. Perhaps the drug overdose is not sufficient to cause death or someone may discover the person before he dies. Many attempted suicides claim that they intended to die; however, no one knows how many completed suicides intended to be saved.

A good example of the gamble in sucide occurs in Tikopia where young people often attempt suicide by swimming far out to sea. The potential suicides can vary the chances of the villagers saving them by their choice of what time to start swimming (late at night or just before dawn), how fast they swim, and in what direction they swim (Firth, 1961).

Female (but not male) attempted suicides have been found to engage in risk-taking behaviors more often than nonsuicidal (psychiatric) patients (Steiner, 1972). Kelley and her associates (1985) devised a questionnaire to assess the tendency of people to engage in behaviors that are detrimental to their welfare (such as failing to buckle seat belts, to have regular dental check-ups, to use condoms, or to eat moderately). Lester and Gatto (1989) found that scores from this questionnaire were strongly associated with suicidal preoccupation in teenagers, especially males.

Thus, it appears that suicidal people may be risk-takers who may also engage in behavior detrimental to their health and welfare.

References

Firth, R. Suicide and risk taking in Tikopia. *Psychiatry,* 1961, 24:1-17.

Kelly, K., Byrne, D., Przybyla, D. P. J., Eberly, C., Eberly, B., Greendlinger, V., Wan, C. K., and Gorsky, J. Chronic self-destructiveness. *Motivation and Emotion,* 1985, 9:135-151.

Lester, D., and Gatto, J. L. Self-destructive tendencies and depression as predictors of suicidal ideation in teenagers. *Journal of Adolescence,* 1989, in press.

Steiner, J. A questionnaire study of risk-taking in psychiatric patients. *British Journal of Medical Psychology,* 1972, 45:365-3274.

Q: Do the methods chosen for suicide vary from year to year?

A: The methods chosen for suicide seem to vary both with their availability and media attention. In effect, there are both long-term trends and short-term fads. The long-term trend in the United States is toward an increasing use of firearms. This is illustrated below:

	Males			Females		
	1960	1970	1980	1960	1970	1980
Firearms	54.2%	58.4%	63.1%	25.3%	30.2%	38.6%
Poisons:						
Solids and liquids	6.9%	9.2%	6.5%	30.1%	36.7%	26.9%
Gases and vapors	11.2%	10.7%	8.2%	7.6%	11.2%	11.7%
Hanging/strangula- tion/suffocation	17.7%	14.6%	14.6%	17.5%	12.1%	10.9%
Other	10.0%	7.2%	7.7%	19.5%	9.7%	11.9%

It is evident that firearms are now the most common method of suicide for men, whose use of firearms has increased steadily over the past two decades. The use of firearms has also grown in popularity among women, so that firearms have now displaced poisoning by solids and liquids as the most widely used method for suicide.

There have also been changes in short-term methods used for suicide. Imitation occurs when a suicide is publicized, leading others to copy that method. For example, suicide by means of car exhaust is increasing dramatically in Great Britain, where cars have no emission controls (Clarke and Lester, 1987). This method was uncommon until the 1980s, when it began to receive media attention. In Zimbabwe, young females have begun to set fire to themselves in recent years (Lester, 1988). In Bergenfield, New Jersey, in 1987, four teenagers killed themselves by means of car exhaust in a garage, and one week later two other teenagers tried to kill themselves with car exhaust in the same garage

(Anon. 1988). (The police finally removed the door to the garage to prevent similar copycat attempts.)

Changes in the availability of potential methods for suicide also affect the frequency of the use of different methods for suicide. For instance, detoxification of domestic gas in England in the 1960s and 1970s reduced its use for suicide. The construction of tall buildings in Hong Kong led to an increase in suicide by jumping, just as the heavy use of pesticides in Sri Lanka and fertilizers in India led to an increase in suicides by poisoning (Farberow, 1975).

References

Anon. Clusters of suicide and attempts. *MMWR,* 1988, 37(14):213-216.

Clarke, R. V., and Lester, D. Toxicity of car exhausts and opportunity for suicide. *Journal of Epidemiology and Community Health,* 1987, 41, 114-120.

Fareberow, N. L. *Suicide in different cultures.* Baltimore: University Park Press, 1975.

Lester, D. Suicide in Zimbabwe. *Central African Journal of Medicine,* 1988, in press.

Q: *Why are some locales so popular for suicide?*

A: Most countries have several sites which are popular for suicide. These places tend to be especially conducive for suicide, usually by jumping or drowning, and have received a great deal of publicity so that they become well known for this purpose. For example, the Golden Gate Bridge in San Francisco is a popular venue for suicide. In the 1970s about 25 people jumped each year. The height of the bridge is sufficiently great that almost all jumpers die.

Seiden and Spence (1983/1984) noted that the Bay Bridge is only six miles away from the Golden Gate Bridge and was completed six months earlier; yet from 1937 to 1979, 672 people jumped off the Golden Gate Bridge, compared to only 121 who jumped off the Bay Bridge. The Golden Gate Bridge allows pedestrians, but counting only non-pedestrians, the Golden Gate Bridge still has more victims (325 verses 107).

Furthermore, East Bay residents who jump off the Golden Gate Bridge have to drive over the Bay Bridge to get there. Fifty percent of East Bay jumpers do this. In contrast, no resident of Marin County has driven over the Golden Gate Bridge to jump off the Bay Bridge. All of the jumpers from outside of California have jumped off the Golden Gate Bridge.

Golden Gate Bridge jumpers are publicized in the newspapers, and tours point out the bridge as a suicide venue. Some people in the San Francisco area bet on which day the next jump will occur. This notoriety keeps Golden Gate Bridge high on the list of suicide sites.

Niagara Falls, well known in former years as the honeymoon capital of America, is also a popular suicide venue. Lester and Brockopp (1971) noted that from 1958 to 1967 an average of 7.1 successful suicides and another 5.7 attempts took place each year.

Abroad, the Eiffel Tower in France and Mt. Fuji in Japan are also well known suicide venues. Recently,

Takahashi (1988) has written about Jukai, a dense forest at the foot of Mt. Fuji, which is the leading site for suicide in Japan with about thirty suicides each year. This forest has an area of ten square miles and is so dense that it is very difficult to see anything in it, and there is no threat that others will intervene. The police and local people conduct searches in the forest for bodies only in the spring and autumn of each year. Jukai received publicity as a suicide venue when a best-selling novel in the early 1960s had the heroine attempt suicide there.

References

Lester, D., and Brockopp, G. W. Niagara Falls suicides. *Journal of the American Medical Association,* 1971, 215, 797-798.

Seiden, R. H., and Spence, N. A tale of two bridges. *Omega,* 1983/ 1984, 3, 201-209.

Takahashi, Y. Aokigahara-jukai: suicide and amnesia in Mt. Fuji's Black Forest. *Suicide and Life-Threatening Behavior;* 1988, 18:164-175.

Q: *Are there geographical differences in the methods used for suicide?*

A: The methods used for suicide vary from region to region in the United States. For example, Marks and Abernathy (1974) found that a greater proportion of suicides used guns in the southern states than elsewhere. In this same vein, Marks and Stokes (1976) surveyed college students in the south and the midwest and found that the southern students were more likely to have had experience with guns when growing up than were the midwestern students. It seems that increased ownership of guns leads to people being more familiar with them and using them for suicide.

Lester and Frank (1988) looked at the use of car exhaust fumes for suicide. They found that the rate of suicide using car exhaust was highest in states where the per capita ownership of cars was higher. They also noted that the northern states had higher rates of suicide from car exhaust than the southern states, but there was no east-west variation. It may be that garages (which permit more privacy during the act of suicide and decrease the likelihood of intervention) are more common in the colder northern states, making car exhaust a more popular method for suicide in this area.

Farmer and Rhode (1980) have documented a wide variation in methods used for suicide in different countries. For example, firearms are used more in the United States and Australia than in other western nations; hanging is used more in Belgium and West Germany; and wrist cutting is used more in Denmark. The authors argue that these differences in methods used for suicide may be responsible for the overall variation in the national suicide rates. The availability of easily accessible methods for suicide in a nation may lead to a higher suicide rate.

References

Farmer, R., and Rhode, J. Effect of availability and acceptability of lethal instruments on suicide mortality. *Acta Psychiatrica Scandinavia,* 1980, 62:436-446.

Lester, D., and Frank, M. L. The use of motor vehicle exhaust for suicide and the availability of cars. *Acta Psychiatrica Scandinavia,* 1988, 78: in press.

Marks, A., and Abernathy, T. Toward a sociocultural perspective on means of self-destruction. *Life-Threatening Behavior,* 1974, 4:3-17.

Marks, A., and Stokes, C. Socialization, firearms and suicide. *Social Problems,* 1976, 23:622-629.

Q: *Is suicide more common in cities or in rural areas?*

A: Many studies have found that suicide is less common in rural areas than in urban areas. This has been reported in the USA (Dublin and Bunzel, 1933), Sri Lanka (Strauss and Strauss, 1953), Hong Kong (Yap, 1958), and Wales (Capstick, 1960). However, discrepant results are published from time to time. For example, Schroeder and Beagle (1953) found a higher rural suicide rate in Michigan.

Investigators see a low rural suicide rate as a result of greater family stability, a larger number of children, and shared social interests, beliefs, and traditions.

The higher suicide rate in cities permits at least three explanations. First, it may well be that the stress of urban life is greater (or of a different kind) than in rural life (for example, there are higher crime rates and more stressful careers in cities); these different stressors may increase the risk of suicide. Second, people in cities are more likely to live alone (or even isolated from others), to be divorced, and to be distant from relatives. These social differences may contribute to the higher suicide rate. Finally, the drift hypothesis argues that those who are psychiatrically disturbed and potential suicides are more likely to migrate (drift) to urban areas, thereby reducing the suicide rate in rural areas while increasing it in the cities. Indeed, studies of the suicide rates of different sections of cities (for example, Maris [1969]), often report that "skid row" sections have the highest suicide rates. (Incidentally, Marris found also that the "gold coast" sections of Chicago had high suicide rates.)

References

Capstick, A. Urban and rural suicide. *Journal of Mental Science,* 1960, 106:1327-1336.

Dublin, L. I., and Bunzel, B. *To be or not to be.* New York: Smith & Hass, 1933.

Maris, R. *Social forces in urban suicide.* Homewood: Dorsey, 1969.

Schroeder, W. W., and Beagle, J. A. Suicide. *Rural Sociology,* 1953, 18:45-52.

Strauss, J. H., and Strauss, M. A. Suicide, homicide, and social structure in Ceylon. *American Journal of Sociology,* 1953, 58:461-469.

Yap, P. M. *Suicide in Hong Kong.* Hong Kong: University of Hong Kong Press, 1958.

Q: *What are Durkheim's four types of suicide?*

A: Emile Durkheim's classification of suicide is perhaps the most cited view of suicide. He proposed that two dimensions of society were critical in determining the society's rate of suicide. First, the degree of social integration was important. Some people are very low in social integration. They have few ties to one another, or those ties they have are weak. This circumstance leads to *egoistic* suicide. At the other extreme, some people are all too integrated into society, so that they feel constrained and even suffocated by the duties and obligations they have toward others. This state of affairs can lead to *altruistic* suicide, where the person kills himself to fulfill obligations to others. The divorced alcoholic, living alone in a room in a decayed section of a city, illustrates an egoistic suicide; the severely ill, elderly relative who feels a burden to his family illustrates an altruistic suicide.

The second dimension that Durkheim proposed was that of social regulation. Some people are highly regulated by the values of the society. Their suicides are an atttempt to free themselves from these pressures and were called *fatalistic* suicide. By contrast, other people are not regulated by the society. They do not share the values of the society and act in their own deviant manner. Such suicides were called *anomic* suicides. Adequate formal tests of this theory have been rare (Masumura, 1977).

In theory it is possible for these two dimensions — social integration and social regulation — to operate independently. For example, a hermit may be low in social integration but still hold the prevailing values of the society, and thus be strongly regulated. In reality, however, studies of societies have found it very difficult to distinguish between these two dimensions. For instance, societies with higher divorce rates are probably lower in social integration and lower in social regulation.

Furthermore, altruistic and fatalistic suicides are rare.

The majority of individual suicides fit more easily into the anomic and egoistic patterns. Thus, Johnson (1965) has suggested simplifying Durkheim's theory of suicide by combining the dimensions of integration and regulation and eliminating consideration of high levels of integration/regulation. The revised formulation then becomes: Suicide is more common in societies where social integration/social regulation is low.

Finally, it must be noted that Durkheim's theory of suicide was originally intended to apply to *societies* or subgroups of societies. However, many investigators have applied it to *individuals*. The validity of this extension is untested.

References

Durkheim, E. *Suicide*. New York: Free Press, 1951.

Johnson, B. D. Durkheim's one cause of suicide. *American Sociological Review*, 1965, 30:875-886.

Masumura, W. T. Social integration and suicide. *Behavior Science Research*, 1977, 12:251-269.

Q: *Is suicide morally right or wrong?*

A: There are four possible answers to this often question. Some believe that people have the inalienable right to do whatever they wish with their own lives: if so, they have the right to kill themselves. At the other extreme, some believe that suicide is murder, and therefore is always wrong, since there is no difference between the murder of someone else and self-murder.

Many people take an intermediate position, believing that some circumstances may make suicide morally right while others make it morally wrong. But what are the circumstances? Buddhism, for example, condemns suicide in many basic writings, yet Buddhist monks in Vietnam during the 1970s found moral justification for immolating themselves rather than harming their persecutors. Islam, too, condemns suicide (and Islamic people have a very low suicide rate), yet Islamic fundamentalists in Iran in the 1980s sacrificed themselves in military missions against the enemy.

At an individual level, we may argue that suicide is morally correct if, for example, the person is already dying from a terminal illness, and he does not physically harm anyone else by his suicidal act, or if some similar criterion is met. (We must be careful here, however, not to confuse the question of morality with the question of rationality. An action may be rational but immoral.) A common set of criteria for making utilitarian moral judgments (that is, based upon the consequences of actions) includes maximizing good and minimizing harm, but these are often subjective judgments.

A final position is to believe that suicide is neither moral or immoral. Rather it is *amoral,* and judgments of right or wrong are irrelevant.

Reference

Battin, M. P. *Ethical issues in suicide.* Englewood Cliffs, NJ: Prentice-Hall, 1982.

Q: *Is committing suicide against the law?*

A: More than 2000 years ago the Greeks ruled suicide to be against the law. They believed that people were servants of the gods, and suicide as an act of rebellion against the gods was punishable. The Athenians considered the hand of the suicidal person that had carried out the act to be a traitor, and cut it off to be buried apart from the body.

The Romans, on the other hand, saw suicide as a personal right of the individual. However, they punished soldiers for suicide, because the act represented desertion; and if a person under indictment committed suicide, the state confiscated his property.

In the early common law of England, sucide was a felony, and the felon was called a *felo de se.* The punishment was burial in a highway with a stake through the body and confiscation of all the person's property. Burial in the highway was abolished in 1823, and confiscation of property, in 1870. In 1961, the British parliament removed suicide and attempted suicide from the list of crimes, although aiding someone else to commit suicide remained a felony.

Although American law is derived mostly from English law, suicide has never been considered a crime in most jurisdictions. Even when suicide has been listed nominally as a crime, no penalties have ever been attached to it. Attempted suicide has been viewed as a crime in some jurisdictions, but the law is invoked rarely and usually only to force a mentally ill person into treatment.

Reference

Dublin, L. I. *Suicide.* New York: Ronald, 1963.

Q: *Do religious beliefs deter people from suicide?*

A: Most of the major religions condemn suicide. Islam, for example, does not approve of suicide (although the suicidal missions in the 1980s of Iranian fundamentalists in the war against Iraq indicate that suicidal behavior is approved under some conditions). Islamic countries have extremely low suicide rates, even allowing for under-reporting in these countries.

Although the Christian religion views suicide as a sin, many countries with very high suicide rates (such as Austria and Switzerland) have predominantly Christian populations. Thus, we must distinguish between the impact of Christianity and the impact of individual religious beliefs.

What we commonly find is that those who are about to commit suicide modify their belief system. Sometimes they come to believe that God will understand their motivations and forgive them. Or they may ask those they leave behind to pray for them to help them avoid some of the anticipated punishment. Perhaps they view the unknown hell that they face as preferable to the known hell that they are experiencing on earth.

However, believing in Christianity has a much broader impact on a person's life than simply affecting certain attitudes toward God. It usually means being involved in the local church and having particular attitudes toward the family and the community. Catholics tend to have large families because of the deliberate avoidance of birth control. Local churches have meetings, festivities, educational programs, charity drives, and other community activities. Thus, in addition to the benefit of faith, being religious also provides an extended social network and decreases the likelihood of divorce or intentionally childless marriages. These factors, perhaps, make religious people less likely to kill themselves.

Breault (1986) studied suicide in the states and counties

of America and found that the extent of church membership in different regions was related to the suicide rate, along with other variables such as the divorce rate and inter-region migration. Thus, stable communities with a high level of church participation and low divorce rates have the lowest suicide rates. Breault also found that county suicide rates were associated with the proportion of Roman Catholics. The more Roman Catholics in a county, the lower the suicide rate.

Reference

Breault, K. D. Suicide in America. *American Journal of Sociology,* 1986, 92:628-656.

Q: *Is suicide ever performed as a duty?*

A: One of Durkheim's four types of suicide is called *fatalistic* suicide because it is committed by a person who is over-regulated by his or her culture. This form of suicide has been observed in different cultural settings.

Hindu religious texts did not originally sanction *suttee*, in which the widow of a deceased husband commits suicide typically by laying down on her husand's funeral pyre (Dublin, 1963). However, priests modified the original teaching to assure people that voluntary death was the surest way to heaven and that, by immolating herself in this way, the widow could atone for the sins of her husband, free him from punishment, and open the gates of paradise to him.

The custom of suttee was facilitated by the fact that no one wanted the burden of taking care of widows, who were often abused and degraded. A wife who refused to commit suttee was threatened with dire punishment. After she killed herself, both families gained enormously in prestige. If she refused, however, especially if she consented but changed her mind, dishonor resulted.

The British in India tried to suppress the custom, formally banning it in 1828. The most incidents in a year took place in 1818, with 839 voluntary deaths. However, cases still occur today in India.

In Japan, *seppuku* (also called *hara-kiri)* is suicide by ritual disembowelment (often followed by an assistant beheading the kneeling suicide). In olden days, some offenders were given the privilege of committing seppuku rather than being executed. Others committed seppuku to make a political protest; the most recent example of which was the ritual suicide of the Japanese novelist Yukio Mishima in 1970 after he had failed to incite a group of soldiers to rise up and restore the Emperor to his former position of absolute, divine monarch.

The tradition of using suicide to atone for mistaken decisions is well established in Japan. After the surrender of

Japan ending the Second World War, about 500 military officers, including the Minister of War, committed suicide (Stokes, 1974). Even today in Japan, the chief executive officer of a corporation will resign and occasionally commit suicide when the company has been accused of dishonorable or nefarious practices.

At the end of the Second World War, over 5000 young Japanese flew their planes or guided small submarines directly into American ships, dying with their craft in the ensuing explosions. (The airmen were called *kamikazes* and the seamen *kaitens.)* Similarly, in the war between Iran and Iraq in the 1980s, many young Iranians committed suicide intentionally as they guided land or sea craft directly at the opposing forces. In some respects these young men chose their actions, but one can also see that their actions were forced upon them by their culture.

References

Dublin, L. I. *Suicide.* New York: Ronald, 1963.
Durkheim, E. *Suicide.* New York: Free Press, 1966.
Stokes, H. *The life and death of Yukio Mishima.* New York: Farrar, Straus & Giroux, 1974.

Q: Why did 900 members of the People's Temple commit suicide in Guyana?

A: The People's Temple was a religious community founded by the Reverend Jim Jones in 1956, based on ideas of fundamentalist Christianity and social activism. The Temple ran nursing homes, clinics and soup kitchens. The community moved to California in 1965, and in 1974 built a utopian community in the South American country of Guyana. In 1978, a U.S. Congressman, accompanied by journalists, visited the community to investigate family complaints of physical and psychological abuse of members.

Jones had been psychiatrically disturbed for some time before the congressman's visit, and he had decided that self-destruction of the community was better than destruction by enemies. On November 18th, 1978, Jones ordered the members of the community to die *en masse*. Vats of poison were prepared and almost all of the members commited suicide. Jones then shot himself.

Neil Smelser (1962), a sociologist, has suggested a way to organize the social variables involved in group behavior. First, the structure of some societies makes collective behavior more possible. The People's Temple was a highly disciplined group of people, dominated by Jones whom they idolized, and isolated from other members of their society (isolated both by beliefs and eventually by geographical location).

Second, tension must occur in the structure. In the months before the mass suicide, the magazine *New West* had published an article on Jones portraying him as brutal, corrupt and mad, and noted that about twenty members had defected. Living conditions were poor with 100-degree temperatures and food shortages.

Next, Smelser proposed that a generalized belief system was needed. Jones persuaded the members of the community that attack was imminent by the CIA, FBI, the Ku Klux Klan, and the Guyanese army, and he staged mock lynchings to illustrate what might happen to them.

Fourth, a precipitating event helps mobilize the people to action. For the People's Temple, this event was the visit of Congressman Ryan with relatives of some of the members of the Temple and journalists. Ryan left after a day, taking several defectors with him. A group of Jones' thugs killed Ryan, some of the newsmen, and a defector.

After this ambush and murder, Jones realized that the Temple truly would be investigated by authorities and disbanded. He called the members together and persuaded them to join together in death.

Finally, Smelser noted that the larger society can occasionally control the group, and that collective behavior typically occurs when this control breaks down or is absent. Social control was absent at Jonestown since the community had intentionally isolated itself from the outside world.

In viewing this mass suicide, psychologists would focus more on the individual personalities of the members of the Temple that led them to idolize and follow a person like Jones. But the members of the Temple are dead, and retrospective study of lives is quite unreliable and inaccurate. Also, when we see that the members of a modern nation like Germany could follow a ruler like Hitler, it suggests that we might not find extreme psychiatric disturbances in the members of the People's Temple.

References

Kilduff, M., and Javers, R. *The suicide cult.* New York: Bantam, 1979.

Smelser, N. J. *Theory of collective behavior.* New York: Free Press, 1962.

Q: *Do suicidal people have below average intelligence?*

A: Very few studies have looked at the intelligence of those who commit suicide, and the few studies that have explored this question have produced inconclusive results.

For example, Reese (1967) studied twenty school-age suicides. Their intelligence test quotients ranged from the low 70s to 147 (100 is average). Ten of the students were doing D and F work while seven were doing A and B work. Another study from the 1960s found higher intelligence-test scores in suicides, while two studies found no significant difference between scores. Only one study has examined this question since then. Shaffer (1974) found that children who killed themselves had above-average intelligence.

Studies of attempted (rather than completed) suicides are even less meaningful, since the results depend so much on how the sample is obtained. Most research on attempted suicide is conducted on patients brought to large municipal (charity) hospitals whose clients are on the whole less educated and of lower socioeconomic class than the average American. Data from these patients, especially on measures of intellectual ability, will be biased.

Looking at the two extremes of inellectual ability—mental retardation and genius—we could argue that completed suicide should be quite rare in the mentally retarded because not only do they lack a mature concept of death, but also they may not have the ability to plan and carry out a decision to kill themselves. On the other hand, the mentally retarded frequently engage in forms of self-destructive behavior, including self-mutilation and mild suicidal gestures.

At the other end of the scale, a common notion about geniuses is that they are psychologically disturbed. Bobby Fischer, perhaps the best chess player the United States has ever produced, seems to illustrate this hypothesis. After he won the world chess championship, he disappeared from public view completely, and reports on his behavior since then portray him as quite eccentric.

If geniuses have a high incidence of psychological disorders it might follow that their suicide rate should also be high. However, a study of gifted children in California who have been followed up for many years has revealed a lower incidence of psychological disturbance than in the general population. Reports on the suicide rate in this group have not yet appeared but will probably be low because the rate of psychiatric disturbance is low.

Reference

Reese, F. D. School-age suicide. *Dissertation Abstracts,* 1967, 27A:2895-2896.

Shaffer, D. Suicide in childhood and early adolescence. *Journal of Child Psychology and Psychiatry,* 1974, 15:275-291.

Q: Do suicide rates go up in wartime?

A: Actually, they go down: available evidence shows that suicide is less common during wartime. For example, during the Second World War, the American suicide rate went down for both civilians and military personnel (Yessler, 1968). This decrease in both sectors is important, for without the parallel reduction in the civilian suicide rate, it could be argued that suicidal soldiers were not recognized as such and were categorized as war casualites. (After all, it is quite easy to get oneself killed by the enemy in a war.)

Rojcewicz (1971) noted that the decrease in suicide rates occurs only during great national wars. (For example, suicide rates did not change in the United States during the Korean War.) Furthermore, the drop in the rate is found in neutral countries too. Rojcewicz felt that an increase in social integration — people feel closer to one another during a crisis — was the major factor responsible for the fall in suicide rates during wartime.

References

Rojcewicz, S. War and suicide. *Life-Threatening Behavior,* 1971, 1:46-54.
Yessler, P. G. Suicide in the military. In H. L. P. Resnick (Ed.) *Suicidal behaviors.* Boston: Little Brown, 1968, 241-254.

Q: *Are risk takers suicidal?*

A: There are many individuals who engage in occupations and hobbies with a high risk of injury and death. Mountain climbers, racing car drivers, and parachute jumpers, for instance, all have an increased risk of death over that of, say, college professors or writers.

Hardly any research has explored the rate of suicide in people who take unusual risks, but a brief report on parachute jumpers noted that of 37 fatalities, ten involved jumpers who failed to pull the ripcord to activate their chutes (Lester and Alexander, 1971). One jumper with experience of over 100 jumps opened his reserve chute at just 50 feet and was killed on impact. In contrast, however, Lester, et al. (1977) found no psychological signs of suicidal motivation in astronaut candidates.

Menninger (1938) thought that the self-destructive impulse could manifest itself in many ways, and he would have judged those who engage in high-risk activities as strongly motivated by unconscious suicidal impulses.

References

Lester, D., and Alexander, M. Suicide and dangerous sports. *Journal of the American Medical Association,* 1971, 215:485.

Lester, D., Kendra, J. M. and Thisted, R. A. Prediction of homicide and suicide. *Perceptual and Motor Skills,* 1977, 44:222.

Menninger, K. *Man against himself.* New York: Harcourt, Brace and World, 1938.

Q: How common is suicide in the United States?

A: The most recent data available for the USA show that the estimated suicide rate in 1986 was 13.1 per 100,000 per year and 12.7 for 1987 (National Center for Health Statistics, 1988). In 1987 there were an estimated 30,980 suicides out of 2,127,000 nationwide deaths. (These estimated are based on a ten percent sample of all deaths.) As such, suicide is the sixth leading cause of death in this country.

Specific rates are available for 1985 as shown below. The following data comes from *Vital Statistics of the United States, 1985:*

Suicide Rate
(per 100,000 per year)

Total	12.3	White males	21.5
		Nonwhite males	11.0
Males	19.9	White females	5.6
Females	5.1	Nonwhite females	2.5

Age:	5- 9	00	Age: 50-54	15.8
	10-14	1.6	55-59	17.0
	15-19	10.0	60-64	16.3
	20-24	15.6	65-69	16.8
	25-29	15.5	70-74	20.7
	30-34	14.9	75-79	23.3
	35-39	14.3	80-84	25.3
	40-44	14.9	85 +	19.1
	45-49	15.5		

The suicide rate appears to have increased during this century, but until 1933 not all states reported death statistics to the federal government. Since the states joining the data collection project in later years tended to be in the west, where suicide rates are generally higher, the overall rate would be expected to rise from 1900 to 1930 simply as a result of these changes. (Alaska and Hawaii had joined the project by 1960.) The suicide rates per 100,000 per year are as follows:

1900	10.2
1910	15.3
1920	10.2
1930	15.6
1940	14.4
1950	11.4
1960	10.6
1970	11.6
1980	

It can be seen that the suicide rate in the USA reached its peak in the 1930s and since then has declined to the present time. The rate has remained relatively constant over the last thirty years.

Reference

National Center for Health Statistics. Annual summary of births, marriages, divorces, and deaths: United States, 1987. *Monthly Vital Statistics Report,* 1988, 36:13.

Q: *Do suicide rates vary from state to state?*

A: There is a wide variation in suicide rates from state to state. In general, the incidence of suicide increases substantially as we move from east to west. In 1980, the rates per 100,000 residents per year were:

AL	11.1	LA	12.1	OH	11.9
AK	16.9	ME	12.5	OK	13.1
AZ	16.9	MD	10.8	OR	14.6
AR	11.6	MA	8.2	PA	11.1
CA	14.5	MI	11.5	RI	11.2
CO	16.3	MN	10.8	SC	9.5
CT	8.9	MS	9.9	SD	12.7
DE	11.9	MO	11.9	TN	12.2
FL	15.4	MT	14.5	TX	12.3
GA	12.6	NE	10.1	UT	13.2
HA	11.4	NV	22.9	VT	14.7
ID	13.1	NH	11.0	VA	13.4
IL	9.3	NJ	7.4	WA	13.3
IN	10.4	NM	17.4	WV	12.5
IA	11.0	NY	9.5	WI	11.7
KS	10.9	NC	11.2	WY	16.0
KY	12.8	ND	11.0		

Note that the lowest incidence of suicide was in the eastern states of New Jersey (7.4), Massachusetts (8.2), and Connecticut (8.9), while the highest rates were in the west — Nevada (22.9), New Mexico (17.4), and Arkansas and Arizona (16.9).

Many studies have searched for particular social characteristics of states that may be associated with (and, therefore, might account for) this variation in the suicide rates. For example, the suicide rates of states have been found to vary with divorce rates, proportion of elderly residents, and population density.

Lester (1988) examined 27 social characteristics of the

states and found that many of the characteristics were strongly associated. One cluster of social characteristics included divorce rates, rates of interstate migration, church attendance, location (east-west), population density, strictness of handgun control laws, and crime rates. This cluster correlated very strongly with suicide rates.

A second cluster included the birth rate, population density, location (east-west), and the percentage who voted in the presidential election for Ronald Reagan. This cluster correlated only weakly with the suicide rate.

On the basis of these analyses, it appears that the variations in the suicide rates of the states may be accounted for in part by indices of social disintegration (such as divorce and migration), and the availability of lethal methods for suicide (such as the strictness of handgun control laws).

Reference

Lester, D. A regional analysis of suicide and homicide rates in the USA. *Social Psychiatry and Psychiatric Epidemiology,* 1988, 23:202-205.

Q: Is suicide more common in communist nations?

A: Hungary has had the highest suicide rate in the world for many years. In 1980 the suicide rate in Hungary was 44.9 per 100,000 per year as compared to only 18.6 per 100,000 in the USA. Bulgaria had a rate of 19.1, Czechoslovakia 30.3 (in 1981), Poland 21.8 (in 1979), and Yugoslavia 20.8. Albania, East Germany, Romania, and the USSR did not report suicide rates for 1980.

However, Lester (1984) has shown that after immigration from these communist nations to the USA (or to Australia), immigrants from Hungary and other communist nations still have the highest suicide rates of the immigrant groups. Furthermore, Hungary and Czechoslovakia had the highest suicide rates in the world before the Second World War when they were not yet communist controlled. (An as-yet unpublished study by Lester shows that the suicide rate decreased in Hungary during the Russian invasion to suppress the liberation movement in 1956.)

These findings suggest that the reasons for the high suicide rates in some of the presently communist countries may have more to do with heredity, child rearing practices, or cultural customs than with the type of government or loss of civil liberties.

Reference

Lester, D. Suicide in communist Europe. *Psychological Reports,* 984, 54:628.

Q: Is suicide common in third world countries?

A: Suicide tends to be less common in third world countries than in more developed nations. The reasons for this, however, are far from clear. First, most third world countries do not report suicide rates (or death rates from any cause) to the World Health Organization. Many of these countries are involved in civil conflict and are extremely poor. Thus, their limited resources are directed to tasks other than accurately classifying and counting deaths.

Very few African nations report suicide rates. Lester has recently calculated suicide rates for Zimbabwe from 1982 to 1984 and found the rate for Africans to be 6.9 per 100,000 per year (1988). This rate is low and similar to that of blacks in South Africa (2.7).

In South America, suicide rates are also quite low. For example, in 1979-1981 Brazil's rate was 3.4 per 100,000 per year; Chile, 5.5; Ecuador, 2.8; Paraguay, 2.7; Suriname, 14.2; and Venezuela, 4.7.

Similarly, the suicide rates reported by Central American countries are low. El Salvador's suicide rate in 1979-1981 was 9.7; Guatemala, 1.0; Mexico, 1.7, and Panama, 2.0.

Several countries in the Middle East have reported extremely low rates, but these results may be misleading. For instance, the Muslim religion condemns suicide, and this strong disapproval may cause suicidal deaths to be hidden or attributed to other causes of death. Thus, the suicide rate in Egypt in 1979-1981 was reported to be only 0.1; Kuwait, 0.7; and Syria, 0.4.

In Southeast Asia, again, very few nations report suicide statistics. Thailand reported to the World Health Organization a suicide rate of 7.1 for 1979-1981. Other sources indicate that Taiwan's rate appears to be 9.9 (Headley, 1983). Apart from these two countries, only the city-states of Hong Kong (12.4) and Singapore (9.8) report suicide rates.

From these data, it would appear that suicide rates are low in third world countries, probably because suicidal deaths are not being counted accurately owing to lack of resources for collecting vital statistics and to the religious disapproval of suicide in some of the nations.

It should be noted, however, that in Israel the suicide rates of immigrants from North Arica and the Middle East are lower than those from Europe and America (Miller, 1976, suggesting that despite the criticism of the accuracy of suicide rates from third world countries, the suicide rates may truly be low.

References

Headley, L. A. *Suicide in Asia and the near east.* Berkeley: University of California, 1983.

Lester, D. Suicide in Zimbabwe. *Central African Journal of Medicine,* 1988, in press.

Miller, L. Some data on suicide and attempted suicide of the Jewish population in Israel. *Mental Health and Society,* 1976, 3:178-181.

Q: *Do immigrants have a high suicide rate?*

A: It has often been noted that immigrants have higher suicide rates than people in the nation to which they have immigrated and higher than people in the nations from which they emigrated. Dublin (1963) presented data in this regard from the United States in 1959/1960.

	Immigrant suicide rate (Per 100,000 per year)	Suicide rate in home nation (Per 100,000 per year)
USA	—	10.6
Austria	32.5	23.0
England & Wales	19.2	11.2
Germany	25.7	18.8
Ireland	9.8	3.0
Norway	23.7	6.4
Sweden	34.2	17.4

It can be seen that the suicide rate of each immigrant group to the USA is higher than the overall USA suicide rate and the suicide rate in its home nation. However, immigrant groups with a higher suicide rate, in general, come from nations with a higher suicide rate; Sainsbury and Barraclough (1968) presented data from eleven immigrant groups in the United States to support this conclusion.

There are several possible explanations for the higher suicide rates of immigrant groups. First, the experience of immigration is very stressful, and this in itself may increase the risk of suicide. Related to this, Lester (1987) found that the greater the number of immigrants from the home nation in the new country, the lower the risk of suicide. A large ethnic population from the home country may make the adjustment to a new environment easier. However, an alternative explanation may be that the psychologically disturbed individuals in the home nations are more likely to want to emigrate.

Interestingly, migration within a country also seems to lead to an increased risk of suicide, although the evidence for this is not as sound as that for immigration.

References

Dublin, L. I. *Suicide.* New York: Ronald, 1963.

Lester, D. Social deviancy and suicidal behavior. *Journal of Social Psychology,* 1987, 127:339-340.

Sainsbury, P., and Barraclough, B. M. Differences between suicide rates. *Nature,* 1968, 220:1252.

Q: *Do primitive societies have low suicide rates?*

A: It has long been thought that suicide was more common in civilized societies (for example, Morselli, 1882). However, this belief has been difficult to test.

In the 1980s, suicide does appear to be more common in developed nations, but it is also true that more developed nations dedicate more resources to the accurate classification and counting of deaths. Also, fewer people die from common infections and treatable diseases in these nations.

However, Lester (1987) found that suicide rates did rise overall in 14 European nations from 1875 to 1975 (from a rate of 7.8 per 100,000 per year to 15.0).

There also appears to be a wide variation of the suicide rates in primitive, nonliterate societies. Hoskin, et al. (1969) reported finding a very high rate of suicide in Kandrian in New Britain (an island off New Guinea) of 23 per 100,000 per year. On the other hand, anthropologists have reported a complete absence of suicide in other primative societies (such as Zūni).

One problem in primitive societies is that the advent of colonial oppression led to great cultural conflicts, resulting in very high suicide rates in some of these societies. For example, Rubinstein (1983) has reported high rates of suicide in recent years in Micronesia. Similarly, some groups of native North Americans are occasionally reported as having high rates of suicide.

It is not possible to go back to the earliest reports of westerners studying these societies to find accurate counts of suicide because those early investigators did not deem it important to make such determinations.

We must conclude, therefore, that there is little evidence that primitive societies in the past had lower or higher suicide rates than civilized societies; today, however, some of these societies do experience extremely high rates of suicide as they try to adjust to modern western culture.

References

Hoskin, J. O., Friedman, M. I., and Cawle, J. E. A high incidence of suicide in a preliterate-primitive society. *Psychiatry,* 1969, 32:200-210.

Lester, D. The stability of national suicide rates in Europe. *Sociology and Social Research,* 1987, 71:208.

Morselli, H. *Suicide.* New York: Appleton, 1882.

Rubinstein, D. Epidemic suicide among Micronesian adolescents. *Social Science and Medicine,* 1983, 17:657-663.

Q: *Are suicides frequently misclassified and "hidden" as accidental or natural deaths?*

A: This is a difficult question to answer, because good cases can be made for both a "yes" and a "no" answer. First let us consider "yes."

It has long been argued that many suicides are misclassified as accidental or undetermined deaths (Dougles, 1967), and instances can be found of police investigation teams and medical examiners clearly ignoring evidence of suicide. Indeed, it has been argued that national differences in suicide rates may be due to such misclassifications. For example, the low suicide rate in Ireland and Northern Ireland as compared to England, Scotland, and Wales has been attributed to misclassification, as have the differences in the suicide rates of Norway, Sweden, and Denmark (Juel-Nielen, et al., 1987).

On the "no" side, it can be noted that national suicide rates stay quite constant despite changes in medical examiners over the years (Lester, 1987). Furthermore, the suicide rates of immigrants from different nations to the united Staes or to Australia are in roughly the same rank order as the suicide rates in the home countries (Sainsbury and Barraclough, 1968). This suggests that suicide rates may be under-reported by nations, but that the degree of under-reporting may be comparable in different nations.

Perhaps we can conclude that instances of suicide are sometimes misclassified through lack of evidence at the

Perhaps we can conclude that instances of suicide are sometimes misclassified through lack of evidence at the inquest or through clear intentions on the part of the officers of the legal system. However, these misclassifications do not appear to be the sole explanation of differences between the suicide rates of nations (or indeed between any groups of the population).

References

Douglas, J. D. *The social meanings of suicide.* Princeton: Princeton University Press, 1967.

Juel-Nielsen, N., N. Retterstol, N., and Bille-Brahe, U. Suicide in Scandinavia. *Acta Psychiatrica Scandinavia,* 1987, 76: supplement 336.

Lester, D. The stability of national suicide rates in Europe, 1875-1975. *Sociology and Social Research,* 1987, 71:208.

Sainsbury, P., and Barraclough, B. M. Differences between suicide rates. *Nature,* 1968, 220:1252.

Q: Can animals commit suicide?

A: Animals die occasionally in ways that, were they humans, might suggest suicidal behaviors. Animals, for example, mutilate themselves, especially if isolated from their peers. Also, some animals seem to waste away when a close partner (or trainer) dies or moves away (Amory, 1970). And, in the best-known example of all, Norwegian lemmings are rumored to perish in large numbers by plunging into the sea on their twice-yearly migrations between their winter and summer habitats.

The issue of suicide in animals has been a subject of debate. Goldstein (1940) asserted that animals could not commit suicide because they did not have a mature concept of death and could not be shown to be willingly seeking that death. (But then, using these same criteria, children, the retarded, and psychotic patients would also be unable to commit suicide.) In contrast, Menninger (1938) felt that the suicidal or self-destructive motive could manifest itself in many indirect, covert, and unconscious ways, and, therefore, animals could commit suicide.

Schaefer (1967) suggested a way to resolve the issue. It must be shown that an animal can discriminate between life and death, can discriminate between a lethal chamber and a non-lethal chamber, and, then, under some circumstances choose the lethal chamber. Schaefer demonstrated the first two possibilities with mice, although not unambiguously. For example, the mice learned the difference between a live and a dead mouse, but Schaefer did not show that they could discriminate between a sleeping or unconscious mouse and a dead mouse, which would have been a more convincing demonstration. However, the mice avoided the lethal chamber.

So the answer to this question depends upon how you define suicide and what you take as evidence for suicide.

References

Amory, C. After living with man, a dolphin may commit suicide. *Holiday*, 1970, May:16-18.

Goldstein, K. *Human nature in the light of psychopathology.* Cambridge: Harvard University Press, 1940.

Menninger, K. *Man against himself.* New York: Harcourt, Brace and World, 1938.

Schaefer, H. H. Can a mouse commit suicide? In E. S. Shneidman (Ed.) *Essays in self-destruction.* New York: Science House, 1967, 494-509.

Q: During which season are suicide rates the highest?

A: It has long been acknowledged that there is a seasonal variation in the rate of completed suicide. Dublin (1963) noted that during the first part of this century the pattern was relatively simple. The peak incidence of suicide occurred in May, and the rate decreased each successive month until the low point was reached in December. This seasonal variation was more marked in rural areas than in urban areas. In recent years, however, the monthly pattern has changed. The peak is still in the spring (May or April) and the low in December, but the variation is less than it used to be, and there are often secondary peaks, as in 1960 and 1964 when there were subsidiary peaks in October.

Dublin noted that the pattern was complicated by the fact that it was not reversed in the southern hemisphere. He found in Australia, for example, that peaks occurred in December and July.

More recent studies have further confused the picture. Lester (1979) studied the incidence of suicide throughout the United States and found peaks in March/May and August/October. Some investigators (for example, Meares, et al., 1981) have claimed a spring peak for both sexes but a fall peak only for females. Skutsch (1981) used this sex difference to provide support for her physiological theory of depressive disorders based on the neurotransmitter dopamine. However, Lester and Frank (1988) failed to confirm a sex difference in the seasonal distribution of suicide in the United States. In addition, Lester (1971) reported that the seasonal distribution of suicide varies with age and with the method used to commit suicide. Overall, it appears that the seasonal distribution of suicide may be much more complex than Dublin originally described.

There has been some speculation on the reasons for the seasonal distribution of suicide, including temporal variations in the weather and social activities. Very little research has been conducted to test possible explanations, although has been conducted to test possible explanations, although Lester and Beck (1974) did find some differences between attempted suicides in the spring versus those in other seasons. For example, spring attempters were less often married and more often agnostics than attempters at other seasons. More research on possible differences is needed before we can fully understand the seasonal variation in suicide.

References

Dublin, L. I. *Suicide*. New York: Ronald, 1963.

Lester, D. Seasonal variation in suicidal deaths. *British Journal of Psychiatry,* 1971, 118:627-628.

Lester, D. Temporal variation in suicide and homicide. *American Journal of Epidemiology,* 1979, 109:517-520.

Lester, D., and Beck, A. T. Suicide in the spring. *Psychological Reports,* 1974, 35:893-894.

Lester, D., and Frank, M. L. Sex differences in the seasonal distribution of suicides. *British Journal of Psychiatry,* 1988, 153:115-117.

Meares, R. Mendelsohn, F., and Milgrom-Friendman, J. A sex difference in the seasonal variation of suicide rate. *British Journal of Psychiatry,* 1981, 138:321-325.

Skutsch, G. Manic depression. *Medical Hypotheses,* 1981, 7:737-746.

Q: Is suicidal behavior affected by the weather?

A: Many claims have been made that the weather exerts an influence on sucidal behavior. Occasional papers have been published which report results suggesting that this might be true. However, Pokorny and his associates have conducted a large number of studies showing that temperature, wind velocity, humidity, atmospheric pressure, rain, thunderstorms, and so on have no impact on the incidence of suicidal behavior (Pokorny et al., 1963). Later studies eliminated sunspots and geomagnetic fluctuations (Pokorny, 1966; Pokorny and Mefferd, 1966).

However, a word of caution is warranted. Pokorny's reseach on weather and suicide was well designed and carried out, but it is based on data only from Texas. Similarly sound studies must be carried out in other regions (and countries) with climates different from that in Texas in order to verify these findings.

It is interesting to speculate on what the underlying mechanism might be if an association between the weather and suicide were confirmed. Could the influence of the weather be directly physiological? Or would it be a result of the impact of the weather on mood, diet, or social activity? No studies have explored the possible explanations for any potential weather influence on suicide.

References

Pokorny, A. D. Sunspots, suicide and homicide. *Diseases of the Nervous System,* 1966, 27:347-348.

Pokorny, A. D., Davis, F., and Haberson, W. Suicide, suicide attempts, and weather. *American Journal of Psychiatry,* 1963, 120:377-381.

Pokorny, A. D., and Mefferd, R. B. Geomagnetic fluctuations and disturbed behavior. *Journal of Nervous and Mental Disease,* 1966, 143:140-151.

Q: *Are suicides more common during the full moon?*

A: Those who work in hospitals and law enforcement agencies often claim that there is an increase in disturbed clients during the period around the full moon. However, sound research has failed to confirm this "lunar effect."

This is also true for suicide. Two studies in the 1960s did not find any association between the number of suicides and the phase of the moon, nor did two studies in the 1970s. However, these four studies all examined relatively small samples of suicides in regional locales.

Lester (1979) reviewed all the suicides in the United States in 1973 and found the average number of suicides was 67.6 on the day of the full moon, versus 67.8 one week later and one week earlier. The new moon also had just the expected number of suicides. Lester extended the time-interval to a three-day period around the full moon and the new moon and found similarly negative results.

On this basis, it must be concluded that there is no association between suicide and the phases of the moon.

Reference

Lester, D. Temporal variation in suicide and homicide. *American Journal of Epidemiology*, 1979, 109:517-520.

Q: *Is there a "blue Monday" effect?*

A: Suicide rates, like homicide rates, vary according to the day of the week. Suicides are more likely on Mondays than on other days; in contrast, homicides are much more likely to take place on the weekends. (It appears as if people murder more during times of leisure, after they have been paid, and while they are relaxing and drinking.)

Lester (1979) found an average of 70 suicides each day in the United States in 1974. The average number on each day of the week was as follows:

Sunday	70	Thursday	68
Monday	76	Friday	69
Tuesday	72	Saturday	66
Wednesday	71		

It can be seen that Monday is the most lethal day of the week, while Saturday is the least. We should note, however, that the differences are quite small in magnitude, but they do indicate a definite trend.

This result is interesting because it tends to confirm a common belief, namely that Monday is the day when people are more likely to have the blues.

Reference

Lester, D. Temporal variation in suicide and homicide. *American Journal of Epidemiology, 1979, 109:*517-520.

Q: Do suicides tend to occur at particular points in our biorhythm cycles?

A: Biorhythms supposedly consist of three cycles—physical, emotional, and intellectual, of 23, 28, and 33 days respectively. During positive phases (the first half of each cycle), an individual's energy is supposed to be high, whereas during negative phases (the latter half of each cycle) energies are supposed to be low. Critical days occur when a cycle crosses the baseline during the switch from a positive to a negative phase. Since there are three cycles, single, double, and triple critical days can occur. During the first 58 years and 68 days of life, there are 4006 single critical days, 312 double critical days, and eight triple critical days, along with 16,926 noncritical days.

Most scientists find no evidence for the validity of biorhythms (Hines, 1979), but a report on 993 completed suicides did find that more occurred on critical days than expected (D'Andrea, et al., 1984). However, Lester (in press) failed to confirm this with a sample of 212 suicides, and so the validity of the earlier study must remain in doubt until more studies appear.

References

D'Andrea, V., Black, D., and Stayrook, N. Relation of the Fliess-Swoboda biorhythm to suicide occurrence. *Journal of Nervous and Mental Disease,* 1984, 172:490-494.

Hines, T. M. Biorhythm theory. *Skeptical Inquirer,* 1979 3(4):26-36.

Lester, D. Biorhythms and the timing of suicide, homicide and natural deaths. *Skeptical Inquirer,* in press.

Q: *Can astrology predict suicide?*

A: Most people tend to equate astrology with Sun signs and horoscopes. There were twelve Sun signs which correspond to the date of birth:

Aries	March 21-April 19
Taurus	April 20-May 20
Gemini	May 21-June 20
Cancer	June 21-July 22
Leo	July 23-August 22
Virgo	August 23-September 22
Libra	September 23-October 22
Scorpio	October 23-November 21
Sagittarius	November 22-December 21
Capricorn	December 22-January 19
Aquarius	January 20-February 18
Pisces	February 19-March 20

The daily horoscopes in newspapers are dervied from these signs.

Several studies have investigated whether those who kill themselves are more likely to have been born under particular Sun signs, but none have found any evidence that this might be so (for example, Lester 1987).

Competent astrologers, however, do not base predictions about people's lives simply on Sun signs. They consider crucial the position of all the planets at the time of one's birth, and include many other, more complex, factors. Furthermore, each sign cannot be considered in isolation, but rather its meaning must be examined in relation to all of the other characteristics of the natal chart.

Only one study has been published on the incidence of suicide according to complete astrological data. Press (1978) compared the complete charts of 311 suicides born in New York City for whom accurate birth data were available with the charts of 311 non-suicidal people born in the same years and in the same boroughs. The natal charts were prepared by computer, and computers were also used to compare each of the many characteristics of the charts (alone and in combination)—a total of almost 100,000 comparisons.

None of the comparisons showed any differences between the natal charts of the suicides and those of the non-suicides!

In addition, eighteen astrologers were asked to compare the complete charts, and only one could differentiate the charts of the suicides and the non-suicides at a rate better than mere guessing.

It appears that astrological characteristics are unrelated to suicide.

References

Lester, D. Month of birth of suicides, homicides and natural deaths. *Psychological Reports,* 1987, 60:1310.

Press, N. The New York suicide study. *Journal of Geocosmic Research,* 1978, 2(2):23-33.

Q: *Is there a "birthday blues" effect for suicide?*

A: Several reports have appeared claiming that people are more likely to kill themselves near their birthdays. Barraclough and Shephard (1976) found that suicides of elderly people took place within 60 days of their bithdays more often than one would expect by chance. Similar results have been reported for children.

Well-known examples of this birthday effect are Ernest Hemingway. who was born July 21, 1899 and killed himself July 2, 1961, and Judy Garland, who was born June 10, 1922 and killed herself June 22, 1969.

This relationship, however, has been challenged recently. Lester (1986) studied 212 suicides in Philadelphia and found no tendency for suicides to cluster near birth dates.

References

Barraclough, B. M., and Shephard, C. Birthday blues. *Acta Psychiatrica Scandinavia,* 1976, 54:146-149.
Lester, D. The birthday blues revisited. *Acta Psychiatrica Scandinavia,* 1986, 73:322-323.

Q: *Does living near electric power lines increase the risk of suicide?*

A: Recent reports have suggested a possible increased risk of certain types of illnnesses among those living near overhead power transmission lines. The thought is that body function may be influenced by the electromagnetic fields. This has led investigators to explore whether suicide might also be more common in those living near power lines.

Only one team of investigators has explored this question. Reichmanis, et al. (1979) reported that the risk of completed suicide was indeed greater among those living near power lines with particular fields (0.10-1.07 and 1.76-2.78 V/m). However, this result needs to be replicated by others before it can be considered a reliable finding.

Reference

Reichmanis, M., Perry, F., Marino, A., and Becker, R. Relation between suicide and the electromagnetic field of overhead power lines. *Physiological & Chemical Physics,* 1979, 11:395-403.

Q: *Do people often commit suicide by jumping in front of subway cars?*

A: In cities with subway systems, committing suicide by jumping in front of an oncoming train is quite common. Guggenheim and Weisman (1974) studied 50 people who used the subway to commit suicide in Boston in the 1960s. Thirty-two of these jumped, six lay down on the tracks, five touched the live wire/rail, and seven wandered along the subway tracks. Most of those who died were the jumpers (16 out of 17).

Before Toronto passed a strict gun control law in 1978, the number of people committing suicide using firearms slightly exceeded the number killing themselves using the subway. After the gun law was passed, these numbers reversed and subway suicides predominated (Rich and Young, 1988).

In the United States in 1985, only 181 people (out of 29,453) committed suicide by jumping or lying before a moving object (which included trains and cars).

References

Guggenheim, F. G., and Weisman, A. Suicide in the subway. *Life-Threatening Behavior,* 1974, 4:43-53.

Rich, C. L., and Young, J. G. Guns and suicide. In D. Lester (Ed.) *Suicide '88 - Proceedings of the 21st Annual Conference of the American Association of Suicidology.* Denver: AAS, 1988.

Q: *Is suicide more common in epileptics?*

A: A good deal of research has been conducted on whether people with abnormal electrical activity in their brains have an increased risk of suicide. In general, the findings have been negative, with two exceptions.

Struve (1986) has found that patients with electroencephalograms showing paroxysmal activity had a higher incidence of suicidal ideation and behavior than other psychiatric patients. In addition, other students have suggested that patients with small, sharp spikes on their electroencephalograms may also have an increased incidence of suicidal ideation and behavior, although even the same investigator was not always able to find this association (Small, 1968, 1970).

But what about epileptics? Two reviews of research on suicide in epileptics have recently appeared. Lester (1988) concluded that the risk of suicide was greater in those with a diagnosis of epilepsy. Barraclough (1981) also reached this conclusion. although Lester felt that there were not enough studies to identify which types of epilepsy carry a higher risk of suicide, Barraclough suggested that the risk was higher for those with temporal lobe epilepsy.

References

Barraclough, B. M. Suicide and epilepsy. In E. H. Reynolds and M. R. Trimble (Eds.) *Epilepsy and psychiatry.* Edinburgh: Churchill Livingston, 1981, 72-77.

Lester, D. *The biochemical basis of suicide.* Springfield: Thomas, 1988.

Small, J. The six per second spike and wave. *Electroencephalography and Clinical Neurophysiology,* 1968, 24:561-568.

Small J. Small sharp spikes in a psychiatric population. *Archies of General Psychiatry,* 1970, 22:277-284.

Struve, F. Clinical electroencephalography and the study of suicidal behavior. *Suicide and Life-Threatening Behavior,* 1986, 16:133-165.

Q: *Are there biochemical indicators of suicide?*

A: This question is of special interest in the 1980s and '90s. Recent years have seen a great resurgence of interest in physiological theories of human behavior, in contrast to the 1960s when researchers focused chiefly on the role of experiences and learning. In line with this trend, there have been many studies of the biochemistry of suicides, and Lester (1988) has recently reviewed this research.

The three major neurotransmitters which might have relevance for suicide are norepinephrine, dopamine, and serotonin. Concentrations of these neurotransmitters and their metabolic breakdown products have been examined in the brains of deceased suicides and in the cerebrospinal fluid, blood, and urine of living suicidal people.

The reliable findings of the research are low levels of serotonin in the central nervous system, low levels of 5-hydroxyindoleacetic acid (the breakdown product of serotonin) in cerebrospinal fluid, and possibly a low norepinephrine/epinephrine ratio in urine. In addition, suicidal involvement is also associated with abnormal responses to the dexamethasone suppression test. In this test, a patient is given a dose of dexamethasone, which causes the pituitary gland to cease production of the adrenocorticotrophic hormone. As a result, plasma cortisol levels should remain low for about 18 hours; however, suicidal people are less likely to show this suppression. Since oral doses of 5-hydroxytryptophan (a precursor of serotonin) stimulate cortisol secretion more in depressed people than in normal people, the abnormal response on the dexamethasone suppression test also suggests the involvement of serotonin in suicidal behavior.

There has been great interest in some laboratories over the possibility that serotonin may also be involved with violent (rather than nonviolent) suicide and with impulsive behavior. However, independent researchers have been unable to replicate these findings consistently.

Although this line of research seems to promise the

possibility of biochemical indicators for suicide, the observed results may simply be a product of the fact tht suicidal people in general are depressed and that the serotonergic system is probably the biochemical basis for depressive disorders. Future research must carefully control for depressive moods and depressive disorders before it can be concluded that these biochemical abnormalities are signs for suicide rather than depression in general. Many psychiatrists, however, now recommend biochemical tests for some patients in order to facilitate an assessment of their suicidal potential.

Reference

Lester, D. *the biochemical basis of suicide.* New York: Springfield: Thomas, 1988.

Q: *Are suicidal people inevitably depressed?*

A: Depression is an ambiguous term. Most often it signifies a type of mood in which a person feels sad, guilty, worthless, and hopeless. It is a mood which most people feel from time to time. Studies have shown that depression is much more severe in suicidal people than in nonsuicidal psychiatric patients (Beck, et al., 1975). Lester, et al. (1979) showed that the higher the suicidal intent of an attempted suicide, the higher the depression score. In addition, those attempted suicides who later went on to kill themselves had the highest depression scores at the time of their earlier attempt at suicide.

However, depression can also refer to a specific psychiatric illness. It is the major symptom in a set of syndromes currently listed under Affective Disorders (in the *Diagnostic and Statistical Manual* published by the American Psychiatric Association). People with a depressive psychiatric illness usually feel depressed, but not all people who feel depressed have a diagnosable psychiatric illness. The evidence is very clear that suicide is much more likely in those who are psychiatrically disturbed.

The psychiatric illness of depression carries the highest risk of suicide. Whereas about one percent of the general population die from suicide, about 15 percent of the deaths of patients with a diagnosis of depressive disorders are from suicide (Guze and Robins, 1970).

Thus, it appears that sucidal behavior is more likely both in those with episodes of severe depression and in those with a diagnosable depressive disorder. Understandably, the scales and indices used to predict risk of suicide give depression the highest weight.

Reference

Beck, A. T., Kovacs, M., and Weissman, A. Hopelessness and suicidal behavior. *Journal of the American Medical Association,* 1975, 234:1146-1149.

Guze, S., and Robins, E. Suicide and primary affective disorders. *British Journal of Psychiatry,* 1970, 117:437-438.

Lester, D., Beck, A. T., and Mitchell, B. Extrapolation from attempted suicide to completed suicide. *Journal of Abnormal Psychology,* 1979, 88:78-80.

Q: *Are there organizations that provide information for people who wish to commit suicide?*

A: Yes, some organizations have been formed to assist those who wish to plan their exit from life in a pleasant manner. In Europe, publications from these groups have on occasion been seized by the authorities who have sought to have the courts declare them illegal, since it is a crime to assist people in commiting suicide.

In the United States, organizations do exist to help people plan a good death (euthanasia); although aiding and abetting suicide is a crime, how-to manuals are protected under the First Amendment. The Hemlock Society—based in Los Angeles* and named after the suicidal action in which the Greek philosopher Socrates killed himself by drinking hemlock—has a newsletter and has published many books. *Let Me Die Before I Wake* gives case histories of desperately sick people who have sought to end their own lives. The book also gives precise doses of medications needed for death.

* P.O. Box 66218, Los Angeles, CA 90066-1871.

Q: *What psychological problems do survivors of suicide face?*

A: All deaths are difficult for survivors, but the problems and the emotions experienced by the bereaved differ for suicides. In suicide, the deceased chose to take his or her own life. This fact has implications about the deceased (for example, was he mentally ill?) and for the survivors (for example, did they drive the person to suicide?).

Many suicidal deaths are unexpected. This creates additional problems which are also faced by survivors of sudden natural, homicidal, or accidental deaths. The survivors are left with unresolved feelings toward the deceased and possibly guilt because there was not time to atone to the deceased for wrongs that may have been done to him.

People in the community often feel quite negatively toward the survivors of the suicide. They act as if the survivors drove the person to suicide or did not respond caringly enough to him when he was alive. When friends of a suicide blame the survivors, additional stress is created and the amount of potential social support during bereavement is reduced. The thought of possible mental illness in the suicide raises the question among friends of whether madness runs in the family, and this too creates a stigma for the family. This stigma is often internalized by the survivors, so that they too worry whether they somehow might have driven the suicide to his death and whether madness runs in the family.

One result of the stress created by a suicidal death is that those related to the deceased may try to deny that the death was suicide. This denial is especially dangerous for the children of a suicide. Denial of the true circumstances of the death makes it impossible for the children to turn to relatives to discuss their thoughts and fears about their parent's death. The problem is made worse by the fact that most neighbors and friends at school do not support the denial and may even taunt the child with the facts of his parent's death.

160

Suicide implies rejection of the survivors. The suicidal act seems to indicate that there was nothing the survivors could have done to help the person. In fact, the suicidal act may even have been planned by the deceased in order to express his anger toward the survivors. For example, he may have shot himself in the head, leaving his spouse and children to find his mutilated body. Or he may have left a suicide note blaming the survivors for his problems.

Finally, the attitudes of officials may be harsher for those who survive a suicidal death than other deaths. The police must investigate and convince themselves that the death was not murder. Insurance representatives may look for ways to avoid paying the death benefits. Ministers and priests may refuse to conduct typical burial services and deny burial in church grounds. These reponses by the community remind the bereaved that the death was not a "natural" one and create an unpleasant situation that the bereaved are ill-equipped to handle.

References

Hewett, J. H. *After suicide.* Philadelphia: Westminster, 1980.
Wallace, S. *After suicide.* New York: Wiley, 1973.

Q: *Can suicide be prevented by making it more difficult for people to obtain the means for killing themselves?*

A: In recent years, evidence has indicated that by making it more difficult for people to kill themselves, the incidence of suicide may be reduced. Three sets of research have focused on this possibility.

First, in studies conducted in Great Britain, the detoxification of domestic gas (in which the carbon monoxide contained in domestic gas was eliminated) was accompanied by a one-third reduction in the British suicide rate (Clarke and Mayhew, 1988). (Not all countries that detoxify their domestic gas have experienced a decrease in the suicide rate, however.) Second, in the USA the reduction of the carbon monoxide in car exhaust as a result of emission controls slowed down the increasing use of car exhaust for suicide in the United States and eventually led to a decrease in this method of suicide (Clarke and Lester, 1987). (In contrast, in Great Britain where there are no emission controls on cars, the use of car exhaust for suicide is increasing dramatically.) Third, research in America has shown that the more firearms available (especially handguns), the higher the suicide rate (Lester, 1984.)

These findings have led to suggestions for ways of preventing suicide, including gun control; placing fences on bridges (like the Golden Gate Bridge in San Francisco, which is a popular venue for suicide); restricting the number of pills in prescriptions of medication and wrapping each pill separately in a plastic blister; prescribing potentially lethal medications (such as anti-depressants) as suppositories (rather than pills); and carefully screening medications to find drugs with low lethality.

A major objection to this concept has been that suicidal people would simply switch to another method for suicide if one method became unavailable. There are a few basic